FEAR NOT!

GOD IS LOVE

FEAR NOT!
GOD IS LOVE

A walk through the book of
Revelation and examination of
God's ultimate conclusion for
humanity

Tom Ziebold

EQUIP PRESS

Colorado Springs

Fear Not! God is Love! A walk through the book of Revelation and an examination of God's ultimate conclusion for humanity

First Edition: 2025
Fear Not! God is Love / Tom Ziebold
Paperback ISBN: 978-1-958585-82-5
eBook ISBN: 978-1-958585-83-2

DEDICATION

This book is dedicated to my prayer warrior. Thanks for all your prayers for our family. The loss of Dad has been difficult. Dad was the cornerstone of our family. He held us all together in his loving arms. His smile felt so warm and comfortable. He always made us feel welcome. Dad welcomed anyone to an open and honest conversation. He always let people know how much they were loved. He was the greatest man I ever knew.

Mom, I know you consistently lift our family in prayer. I want you to know how much we all appreciate and love you. Your prayers have helped us through the grieving process.

Dad wants you to know when we meet him again in heaven he will be completely healed and will be able to walk again without pain. I can't wait for that day when we can all be together again in Heaven. Dad always looked after you and cared for you. He loved you more than you will ever know. You were his world. He wants you to know now, while you are still grieving, how much he loves you. He also wants you to be strong and know Jesus is taking care of you while he's away. Have no fear, Mom, you're in the loving embrace of Jesus.

Your family needs you. You've always been our prayer warrior. We all need your prayers. Life has been tough on all of us since dad passed away. Rest assured; God hears your prayers. Even though sometimes you feel like they aren't being answered, your loving father will answer them in due time. I know I speak for everyone in our family when I say that I can't wait to be reunited with dad where we will, once again, see his incredible smile. Fear not, mom, God loves you.

This book is also dedicated to my fellow followers

in Christ. To those who have accepted Jesus as their savior and Lord of their lives, to those that have an earnest desire to read and study God's word, and those who whole heartedly believe the sacrifice Jesus made on the cross for the atonement of our sins is the only way we are pardoned from living a life of sin. This book is dedicated to those that understand it is through this recognition and our acceptance of Him as our savior that we can come into a loving relationship with our living God. This book is dedicated to those people that have chosen to be the hands and feet of God. Those who have chosen to take on active roles within the great commission Jesus has challenged us and blessed us with. This book is dedicated to those people earnestly seeking to stay connected to the vine, and those people earnestly seeking to understand and live by the Godly purpose God has blessed you with.

My prayer for you is you will be blessed in some way from reading the pages of this book, and you would be challenged to continue upon the Godly path Jesus has laid out ahead of you. I pray for you to remain connected to the vine, and that your thirst for knowledge and truth are met through the active study of God's word, and listening and obeying the promptings received through the Holy Spirit.

ACKNOWLEDGEMENT

Unless otherwise noted, Bible references in *Fear Not! God is Love* are drawn from the World English Bible, a public domain translation in draft form. For more information on this please see *https://worldenglish.bible/.*

TABLE OF CONTENTS

FORWARD

I'M A PROJECT MANAGER. I have no formal background in religion or theology, but I was raised in a home that openly anticipated God's answers to prayer. My mother actively shared her prayer life with me while I was growing up. She practices the art of prayer journaling. Journaling allows her to see the outcomes of her prayers over time. Her dedicated practice in prayer journaling enables her to recognize a lot of God's miraculous answers to prayer. I am a firm believer we serve a God who is still actively in the business of performing miracles.

I know this to be true because my family experienced a miracle when I was very young (about 2 years old). We experienced a terrible house fire. This was before smoke detectors were required on every floor of the house. The fire took place in the early morning when everyone was asleep upstairs. By the time my mother realized the house was on fire it was fully engulfed in flames. We barely escaped with our lives.

The house fire occurred at a time when we were litigating a court case to obtain more financial support for my grandmother. To obtain more financial support for her it was necessary to prove her husband was no longer living. We had the necessary legal documents to prove he had passed away inside the chest drawer located in our dining room. My mother knew we needed those documents, and we didn't have time to replace them prior to our court hearing. Immediately upon exiting the house My mother quickly ran to a neighbor and called the church prayer chain. She asked them to pray for the protection of the dining room. She told them we had important documents in one of the chest drawers in that room of the house. Those documents needed to be protected through the fire. The house was destroyed except for one room (the dining room). Exploring the house in the aftermath of the fire revealed evidence of the miracle God performed that evening. The wax candles on the dining room table didn't even melt! In addition, the important documents our family needed were completely unharmed. The documents had no evidence of water or smoke damage!

Exploring the aftermath of the fire further allowed us to see examples of just how hot the fire was. My mother found a metal jewelry case melted around a watch that had been inside the case. In addition, the floor of the living room (the room adjacent to the dining room) fell through

1

to the basement, and one of the fire trucks that was parked too close to the house sustained heat damage. The firemen that helped put out the blaze said it was one of the most intense house fires they had ever seen. This was a hot fire, and yet the candles sitting on the dining room table didn't even melt! There is no question God answered the prayers of the church prayer chain that evening. We can have confidence the God we serve today is the same God who performed miracles in the Bible. Our God is still in the active business of performing miracles today on behalf of His believers. He accomplishes them today through answered prayers.

Are you looking for something that can make you feel more grounded in what has become a chaotic world? Are you looking for something you can rely upon as truth to help guide you through a world that seems to have thrown truth out the window? I always find security in speaking to God through prayer, reading God's word, and listening to the prompts of the Holy Spirit. Why not look to a God that is still actively performing miracles for your security? My earnest prayer is that you are blessed in some way from reading the pages of this book. I pray the pages of this book help you in your quest for guidance, truth, and security.

WRITING THE BOOK

WE SERVE A GOD WHOSE very nature is love. This is awesome news for us, and yet many still doubt God's ability to care for our needs. I personally struggle with doubt even though I've seen direct examples of God's miraculous answers to prayer in my life. I've experienced times in my life where I have been anxious and reluctant to move forward on something I think God has put on my heart. One such example is God giving me the feeling to write this book. You see, I previously authored another book documenting the many amazing answers to prayers provided to my mother from her prayer life. I couldn't find a publisher for the book, but I still felt the book needed to be published. I made the decision to self-publish the book. My first book was viewed as a failure in the eyes of those closest to me. I spent about $10,000 self-publishing the book, but it simply didn't sell. Ultimately the book was removed from circulation.

You can imagine when I started to get feelings leading me to write another book, doubts crept in. I really felt like God wanted me to write this book, but I was anxious about starting the project given my previous perceived failure. I went back and forth in my mind, started an outline, and doubts crept in about the story. Would it be a good book? Would people really want to read it? I was really struggling. I prayed to the Lord, "God, if you want me to author this book, you're going to have to send me some sort of sign." That day I worked on the title of the book. I made the determination it should be *Fear Not! God is Love*. Later in the day I drove up to visit my mother (to talk about the book project with her). On my way to my mother's house, I noticed a car behind me driving a bit erratically in my lane of traffic. The car drove up and got closer to me and swerved a bit into the other lane of traffic. The car swerved enough to make me nervous and I moved out of the way of the car to allow him to pass. After passing me the car swerved back into my lane again and was right in front of me. I noticed the bumper stickers on the car. The bumper stickers read "God is Love!" and "God Loves You!" Those bumper stickers were so close to the title of my book I felt this had to be a sign from God. I felt an immediate surge in my soul! I quickly pulled my phone out of my pocket. I took a picture of the car so I might not forget God's sign to me. Whenever I need a reminder that God wants me to continue to work on this book project, I simply look at that picture. I recognized this as a sign to continue working on the book you hold in your hands today.

When Christians are in doubt, when we need an answer, we should ask God for guidance. It's perfectly acceptable for us to ask for a sign from God. Sometimes He will provide the sign in a truly unexpected way. If we ask for a sign, we must be actively looking for His answer and we must expect that sometimes He will give us an answer in a way that you didn't expect. This is one of the reasons my mother keeps a journal of her prayer life.

By recognizing the answered sign, I am more confident than ever God wanted me to author my second book. I started writing and out-lining the chapters in earnest. I don't know what the impact of this book will be. If the book completely flops again, I will likely be out some more money. I might face some ridicule again in my own family, but I firmly believe God's purpose for this book is to bring glory to Him by showing He is a God of mercy, justice, and love.

I also think it's important to point out we shouldn't measure the im-pact of something God is asking us to do strictly from a financial perspec-tive. God knew my doubts about writing this book. He knew some of the closest people to me in my own family viewed my first book as a complete failure. Knowing my many doubts, God gave me a sign my first book wasn't a failure in His eyes. You see, I was in the hospital for over a week. The sudden hospitalization forced me to take a break from working on this book project. While in the hospital I met a man, and we began to talk. I told him I was in the process of writing a religious book. I shared with him some of my doubts and the perceived failure of my first book. He asked me for the title of my first book. I told him "The Hand of the Holy Spirit – Miraculous Answers to Prayer." His eyes lit up. He said, "Oh, my God! My wife loves your book!" Further, he said, "That book saved her niece who, before reading the book, was an atheist." At that moment in the hospital, I felt another surge in my soul. It was the same feeling I had after seeing the bumper stickers on that car. I firmly believe God orches-trated the circumstances that placed me in the hospital so He could show me my first book was a success in His eyes. I felt humbled to know His vi-sion of success centered around the impact the book had on spreading His message to those that needed to hear it. It had nothing to do with financial success in human standards. God permitted me to see a small glimpse of the impact my first book made in the lives of a few people, and I thanked Him for providing the acknowledgement to me. This served as a second sign God wanted me to continue with this book project.

A GOD CENTERED LIFE

I FIRMLY BELIEVE WE LIVE in a world today where many Christians have a thirst for knowledge and understanding. The world we live in today has become more and more corrupt. We see the influence of the secular world and the world view all around us. The media chooses to convey a constant narrative about how we should live to please ourselves and seek immediate gratification. We live in a world that promotes consumerism, selling us goods we don't need and sending us a message that it's not only acceptable for us to purchase those goods, but we deserve them now, and we should do whatever is necessary to obtain them. After all, the world tells us we only have one life to live, so why not enjoy this life to the fullest now? Why not get as much as we possibly can in this life to maximize our enjoyment here and now? The world teaches us to live the best life we can possibly live while we are young, to enjoy our youth while we can, even if it means going into debt, so we can maximize our enjoyment. After all, the world tells us we may not be able to enjoy the fruits of our labor as much in old age, so it's fine to go into debt to enjoy those things while we are young enough to fully take advantage of them.

You, as a born-again Christian, know there is another way. You know this deep down in your soul. God's message in the Bible teaches us to live another way. It teaches us to avoid the trappings of what the world has to offer, to live within our means, and to be generous to others as God has shown generosity to you. You know deep within your soul that we are to stay connected to God through studying His word and giving Him time in our devotions and prayer lives so we can have an active, open, and consistent communication to Him through prayer and through the Holy Spirit. You know deep down in your soul what God desires of you and yet, many of us simply don't live our lives this way. We get too busy in our lives to really take the time to truly spend dedicated time with Him through the study of His word. The book of Revelation describes many churches, and the Bible paints a picture of the church that will exist in the end times. It paints a picture of churches being neither hot nor cold for God's message. It paints a picture of churches that know about God, and His message of the gospel, but are no longer truly relying upon Jesus for their every need. It paints a picture of churches who have become comfortable and complacent in the world around them. I ask you to take a good look at most Christian churches around us today and ask yourself, honestly, how closely this aligns with what we see today. God tells us that He will spew out of his mouth those that follow Him in this way. We, as Christians, need to be aware of this fact and we must actively work to make sure we don't become comfortable and complacent in serving the Lord in our world today.

I firmly believe we serve a God today that is still in the active business of performing miracles for His followers. God performs miracles for those people who remain earnestly connected to the vine, and who actively follow Him and have Him in the center of their lives. These are those that can truly call Jesus their LORD and savior. They not only see Him as their savior, but they also live a life where He is at the very center. He is truly their Lord! These are the true followers of Christ, those that truly seek to be His hands and feet of this world. They are generous with their time and resources. They actively get involved filling the needs of those around them, and they stay diligently connected to God through active and consistent study of His word. As born-again Christians, don't we all really want this deep down in our soul? Once you accept Jesus as your lord and savior, He gives you the Holy Spirit to guide you. That desire deep within your soul to live this way is the Holy Spirit speaking to you, nudging you, and prompting you to live with Him at the very center of your life. It doesn't come naturally for us, we all have a natural desire toward the secular world, toward consumerism, and toward pride and greed, but the feelings you have deep within your soul to live a life truly connected to God, your creator, will never go away once you have accepted Jesus as your savior. I would encourage you to pray about it and take the necessary steps away from the things this secular world has to offer and take the active step toward a place in your life where you place God at the very center of everything you do.

I decided a few years ago to change the way I was living. I was a born-again Christian, and I was actively going to church, but I wasn't staying really connected to God. God challenged my heart to make some changes in my Christian walk to really put him at the center of my life. He challenged me to obtain a better understanding of what His godly purpose was for my life, and he challenged me to remain consistently connected to Him through the study of His word and to listening to the prompts of the Holy Spirit. He challenged me to go immediately where those prompts lead me and start living a more generous life. I found when I started to move in the direction God was asking me to move I felt more peace than I have ever felt before. I felt peace within my soul, and I felt God leading me more and more into His word.

If you are feeling some of these same promptings I have described, I would encourage you to make the changes the Holy Spirit is encouraging you to make. I firmly believe if you make those changes in the way you serve Him, to truly put Him at the center of everything within your life, you will truly be blessed by Him. These blessings are bestowed to those that take active steps within their faith. God promises you many blessings within the Bible for those that fully place God at the center of their lives. In fact, God tells us to test Him in His generosity when we live this way. He tells us He will pour out so many blessings upon us we won't be able to store them. I have found sometimes the blessings God is providing us aren't necessarily financial in nature, but there is so much peace in living the way God truly challenges us to live I would encourage everyone reading this book if you feel these promptings give Him more time and place Him at the center of your lives immediately if possible. I found once I started living my life the way God was asking me to (with Him at the very center) I found more peace and gratification than ever before.

God makes many promises in the Bible regarding how He will bless Christians who live their lives with Him at the very center. God knew that often one of our last holdouts in our Christian Walk with him is to surrender our finances to Him (I know this is where I most personally struggle). God tells us to bring the full tithe into His church. He tells us to do this to ensure we make Him the very center of our lives. The Bible communicates we cannot serve two masters. We cannot serve money and God. God doesn't need your finances, but He wants your hearts, and for many of us He knows that what we hold onto most tightly is our finances. We do this because we fail to truly trust Him, that He will provide graciously for every need through his vast resources. Malachi chapter 3 provides the promise God has offered to those that truly test Him with their generosity, but this chapter also describes and provides a warning to those who don't truly live their lives in this manner, offering the first fruits of what He has provided them back to God. It is worth reading the entire chapter of Malachi 3 to gain a full understanding of both God's promise and warning.

MALACHI CHAPTER 3:

"Behold, I send my messenger, and he will prepare the way before me; and the Lord, whom you seek, will suddenly come to his temple; and the messenger of the covenant, whom you desire, behold, he comes!" says Yahweh of Armies. "But who can endure the day of his coming? And who will stand when he appears? For he is like a refiner's fire, and like launderers' soap; and he will sit as a refiner and purifier of silver, and he will purify the sons of Levi, and refine them as gold and silver; and they shall offer to Yahweh offerings in righteousness. Then the offering of Judah and Jerusalem will be pleasant to Yahweh, as in the days of old, and as in ancient years. I will come near to you to judgment; and I will be a swift witness against the sorcerers, and against the adulterers, and against the perjurers, and against those who oppress the hireling in his wages, the widow, and the fatherless, and who deprive the foreigner of justice, and don't fear me," says Yahweh of Armies. "For I, Yahweh, don't change; therefore you, sons of Jacob, are not consumed. From the days of your fathers, you have turned away from my ordinances, and have not kept them. Return to me, and I will return to you," says Yahweh of Armies. "But you say, 'How shall we return?' Will a man rob God? Yet you rob me! But you say, 'How have we robbed you?' In tithes and offerings. You are cursed with the curse; for you rob me, even this whole nation. **Bring the whole tithe into the storehouse, that there may be food in my house, and test me now in this," says Yahweh of Armies, "if I will not open you the windows of heaven, and pour you out a blessing, that there will not be room enough for.** *[emphasis added]* I will rebuke the devourer for your sakes, and he shall not destroy the fruits of your ground; neither shall your vine cast its fruit before its time in the field," says Yahweh of Armies. "All nations shall call you blessed, for you will be a delightful land," says Yahweh of Armies. "Your words have been stout against me," says Yahweh. "Yet you say, 'What have we spoken against you?' You have said, 'It is vain to serve God;' and 'What profit is it that we have followed his instructions, and that we have walked mournfully before Yahweh of Armies? Now we call the proud happy; yes, those who work wickedness are built up; yes, they tempt God, and escape.' Then those who feared Yahweh spoke one with another; and Yahweh listened, and heard, and a book of memory was written before him, for those who feared Yahweh, and who honored his name. They shall be mine," says Yahweh of Armies, "my own possession in the day that I make, and I will spare them, as a man spares his own son who serves him. Then you shall return and discern between the righteous and the wicked, between him who serves God and him who doesn't serve him.

I've decided to share this book with you because I want to share some insights that I have had through studying God's word. The Bible tells us in the end times God will send a great deception on this world that could deceive even His elect. I think we, as born-again, Christians need to be aware of this and we need to do everything we can to stay connected to Him through the active study of His word so we can guard against being misled by the many deceptions the world will provide to us during the end times. I firmly believe we are participating in the end times ministry, and we, as Christians, really need to understand the danger of not staying connected to the vine during these times and not truly putting God at the very center of our lives, to truly govern every aspect of our lives. You will see in the pages of this book that during the end times many around the world will be deceived. They will truly believe they are following the one true God when, in fact, they are following a great lie (the great deception). The people who are being deceived will see the fulfillment of many miraculous signs and what they believe will be the holy fulfillment of prophecy which will lead them to believe, beyond a shadow of a doubt, they are following the one true God. The very deceptions that will be used to mislead humanity are called out within pages of the Bible and my intent in bringing this book to you is simply to call them to the surface so you may be able to see the truth of God's word.

The fact of the matter is everything centers around the basic and simple message of the gospel. Everything about your salvation hinges upon what you believe about Jesus Christ. The Bible clearly communicates Jesus died on the cross and was resurrected from the dead so He would become a perfect sacrifice and atone for all of humanities sins. The great deception will seek to deliver a message that communicates Jesus never died on the cross for you, He never rose from the dead, and

He, therefore, never atoned for your sins. This is the great lie that will be communicated in the great deception that will be provided to the world during the end times. It's important that you, as a born-again Christian know, beyond a shadow of a doubt, that Jesus did, in fact, die on the cross for you. He died as a perfect sacrifice for the atonement of your sins, and He rose from the dead and now sits at the right hand of God, the Father. Everything else in this book hinges upon that simple understanding. You will see within the pages of this book why it is so important that born-again Christians absolutely hold to this core belief beyond all others. My prayer for everyone reading this book is that you would come away with that very simple understanding and that you would truly accept Jesus as your lord and savior.

WHITE LEATHER SANDALS

MY MOTHER CONVEYED A STORY with me about serving in her early church life. This story has always resonated with me, as it speaks to God's providence in providing people with guidance from the Holy Spirit to help provision those with specific needs in our community. I will convey the story from her point of view, as that is how the story was conveyed to me as a child early in my Christian Walk with Jesus.

While I was living in Cincinnati, I became very active in church. Mark drove a bus route through Forest Park, picking up children to take them to church each Sunday. Another member of the church, Mary, and I would walk the bus route, going door to door, asking people if they would send their children to church each week. We invited young people to attend our church services each week. Many of these young people didn't have parents who were active in church, so the only way for them to attend the church services was to ride the church bus that Mark drove.

I had been noticing a pair of white leather sandals at a shoe store near my house. The sandals were beautiful, and I fell in love with them. The only problem was the sandals were half size too small for me. For some reason I decided to buy the sandals even though they didn't exactly fit my feet and were uncomfortable for me. I guess I figured the sandals would eventually stretch to fit my feet because they were made of leather. One morning, on my way to pick up Mary, I decided to put the sandals in the car. I picked up Mary and we rode together in my car to the neighborhood that we were going to walk that day. As we were walking the bus route, we came across a house. We asked the lady of the house if she would permit her three children to attend church services by riding the bus. The lady granted permission, but her daughter, who was probably thirteen or fourteen years old, refused to go. She seemed to be embarrassed, so I asked her what she was embarrassed about. The girl said, "I would attend your church services, except that I don't have a pair of good shoes to wear to church. I would be embarrassed to attend church in any of the shoes I have."

At that moment I knew exactly why I had brought those shoes along with me in the car that day! It became clear to me why I had purchased those shoes in the first place! Those shoes, that were half size too small for me, were never intended for me! They had caught my eye in the shoe store, and the Holy Spirit impressed me to buy the shoes even though they didn't fit. I knew those shoes would be exactly the right size for this little girl. I looked down at the girl's feet and asked her what size shoe she wore, even though I already knew the answer in my own mind. Amazingly, her shoe size was the same size as the white sandals that I had brought with me that day! I knew, without a doubt, the purpose for those white leather sandals. The Holy Spirit knew what this little girl needed before she had to even ask for it! I told her that I just happened to have a brand-new pair of white leather sandals in my car and that she should consider these a gift from God. The Holy Spirit intended these sandals for her, and I was supposed to give them to her. I got the sandals from my car, gave them to the little girl, and asked her if she would attend our church service. She said she would.

This little girl and her family regularly attended our church services for quite some time. In fact, they were still attending church on a regular basis after I moved to Michigan. They became active in all parts of the church service. James 1:17 says, "Every good and perfect gift is from above, coming down from the Father of the heavenly lights, who does not change like shifting shadows."

Matthew 6:25-30 says the following:

> Therefore, I tell you, do not worry about your life, what you will eat or drink; or about your body, what you will wear. Is not life more important than food, and the body more important than clothes? Look at the birds of the air; they do not sow or reap or store away in barns, and yet your heavenly Father feeds them. Are you not much more valuable than they? Who of you by worrying can add a single hour to his life? And why do you worry about your clothes? See how the lilies of the field grow. They do not labor or spin. Yet I tell you that not even Solomon in all his splendor was dressed like one of these. If that is how God clothes the grass of the field, which is here today and tomorrow is thrown into the fire, will He not much more clothe you, O you of little faith?

God provides for His people. He knows their needs before they even ask for them. Oftentimes He has already provided for their need before they even know about it!

FEAR NOT! GOD IS LOVE!

> For God didn't give us a spirit of fear, but of power, love, and self-control. ~ **2 Timothy 1:7**

> I can do all things through Christ, who strengthens me. ~ **Philippians 4:13**

THE BIBLE PROVIDES 365 VERSES that tell us to "Fear Not." We are provided one Bible verse for each day of the year! God does not want us to walk in fear, but instead, He wants us to walk in confidence and strength, relying on His power.

Consider this passage from John's first letter:

> Beloved, let's love one another, for love is of God; and everyone who loves has been born of God, and knows God. He who doesn't love doesn't know God, for **God is love**. By this God's love was revealed in us, that God has sent his one and only Son into the world that we might live through him. In this is love, not that we loved God, but that he loved us, and sent his Son as the atoning sacrifice for our sins. Beloved, if God loved us in this way, we also ought to love one another. No one has seen God at any time. If we love one another, God remains in us, and his love has been perfected in us. By this we know that we remain in him and he in us, because he has given us of his Spirit. We have seen and testify that the Father has sent the Son as the Savior of the world. Whoever confesses that Jesus is the Son of God, God remains in him, and he in God. We know and have believed the love which God has for us. **God is love**, and he who remains in love remains in God, and God remains in him. In this, love has been made perfect among us, that we may have boldness in the day of judgment, because as he is, even so we are in this world. There is no fear in love; but perfect love casts out fear, because fear has punishment. He who fears is not made perfect in love. We love him, because he first loved us. If a man says, "I love God," and hates his brother, he is a liar; for he who doesn't love

his brother whom he has seen, how can he love God whom he has not seen? This commandment we have from him, that he who loves God should also love his brother. ~ *[emphasis added]* **1 John 4:7-21**

These verses clearly say, "God is love." They don't say "God loves." They say, "God *is* love." This distinction is important because the very essence of God is being equated to Love. There is no shadow of hate in God. Let's look closely at verses 10-11 again, which provide the very definition of love:

This is love, not that we loved God, but that he loved us, and sent his Son as the atoning sacrifice for our sins. Beloved, if God loved us in this way, we also ought to love one another.

Even when we had no love for Him, He still loved us so much that He sacrificed His Son on the cross to make a path for us to be saved and return to Him. Solely because of this, God expects you to love other people. Nobody is perfect. We have all fallen short of the glory of God. We all have committed sins that required Jesus' blood to cover them. It is the sacrifice that Jesus made on the cross that enables us to enter a relationship with a perfect God. Further, these verses state we are to actively love *everyone*. If anyone is in need let us do everything possible to satisfy their need. Finally, in verse 17, the definition of love is given: "His love is made complete in us." We are to be the hands and feet of Jesus. We must show His love by carrying it actively to others in the world. That is the only way His love is made complete in this world. The comfort I take from these Bible verses is the confidence that I serve a God whose very nature is love. When I'm looking at Bible verses, I apply that lens to everything I read.

Do you become frightened when reading the book of Revelation? That book really frightens me. The book of Revelation talks about world wars, huge percentages of the earth's population dying, cataclysmic events, meteor strikes on the earth, oceans and rivers turning to blood, and all the ocean life dying out. How can someone not be terrified when reading these words in the book of Revelation?

At some point a few years ago, God spoke to my heart. He challenged me to really take another look at the book of Revelation. He led me to look at it from a different perspective. He wanted me to look at the book from the perspective that He is love. Everything He does is a loving act for those that believe in Him and follow Him. He challenged me to re-read the book of Revelation and focus on the fact that He is a loving God. Everything He does has a component of Love associated with it for those that believe in Him.

God doesn't want His believers to be afraid of anything. I took the challenge to heart and started again through the book of Revelation. When I applied the lens of "God is love" my entire perspective changed. I now view the *entire* Bible through that same lens. My approach in reading the Bible has changed entirely. That's one of the reasons I wrote this book. I want to share my experience with you in hope that it may be beneficial to you and change the way you approach and study the Bible: to understand that everything you read within the Bible must be approached with the idea that God is love.

If the book of Revelation frightens you, I would encourage you to take another look at it and view things through a different lens. Look through the lens of trying to find good in everything for those that believe in God. You serve a God whose very essence is love. Understand He works good in all things for the benefit of those who believe in Him. Anyone who believes in the sacrifice Jesus made on the cross is a follower of God, and He works everything to your ultimate benefit. He brings good out of bad events for those who follow Him. As followers of God, we can live without fear, because the Bible says perfect love casts out all fear.

> There is no fear in love; but perfect love casts out fear, because fear has punishment. He who fears is not made perfect in love.
> **~ 1 John 4:18**

The phrase "perfect love" here speaks directly to God's nature. He is love. Understanding this truth builds faith. You should have no fear in anything you do in His honor. God reveals His truth to us through His word and the Holy Spirit, so we may not be anxious or afraid in the days that lie ahead. God is love. You should have no fear in approaching Him.

GOD'S PERFECT JUSTICE

> You, son of man, tell the house of Israel: 'You say this, "Our transgressions and our sins are on us, and we pine away in them. How then can we live?"' Tell them, '"As I live," says the Lord Yahweh, "I have no pleasure in the death of the wicked; but that the wicked turn from his way and live. Turn, turn from your evil ways! For why will you die, house of Israel?" ~ **Ezekiel 33:10-11**

THIS PASSAGE FROM EZEKIEL TELLS us He takes no pleasure in the death of the wicked. It is God's desire that we all turn from our evil ways and repent (return) to Him rather than remain on our wicked path and die. Just a few verses later Ezekiel describes the fall of Jerusalem and explains the cause of Judah's ruin:

> In the twelfth year of our captivity, in the tenth month, in the fifth day of the month, one who had escaped out of Jerusalem came to me, saying, "The city has been defeated!" Now Yahweh's hand had been on me in the evening, before he who had escaped came; and he had opened my mouth, until he came to me in the morning; and my mouth was opened, and I was no longer mute. Yahweh's word came to me, saying, "Son of man, those who inhabit the waste places in the land of Israel speak, saying, 'Abraham was one, and he inherited the land; but we are many. The land is given us for inheritance.' Therefore tell them, 'The Lord Yahweh says: "You eat with the blood, and lift up your eyes to your idols, and shed blood. So should you possess the land? You stand on your sword, you work abomination, and every one of you defiles his neighbor's wife. So should you possess the land?"' "You shall tell them, 'The Lord Yahweh says: "As I live, surely those who are in the waste places will fall by the sword. I will give whoever is in the open field to the animals to be devoured; and those who are in the strongholds and in the caves will die of the pestilence. I will make the land a desolation and an astonishment. The pride of her power will cease. The mountains of Israel will be desolate, so that no one will pass through. Then they will

know that I am Yahweh, when I have made the land a desolation and an astonishment, because of all their abominations which they have committed." - **Ezekiel 33:21-29**

What caused the destruction of Judah? The verses above clearly state that Judah is responsible for its own destruction. God provided them so many merciful warnings—they should have repented. Judah chose not to repent, so God ultimately permitted their destruction. God is innocent of the fall of Jerusalem. Jerusalem fell due to its own sin and failure to repent. They relied on their own strength and worshiped idols. They failed to worship and give glory to their one true God. This is the reason God permitted their destruction.

Ezekiel 33:18-20 says the following, "When the righteous turns from his righteousness, and commits iniquity, he will even die therein. When the wicked turns from his wickedness, and does that which is lawful and right, he will live by it. Yet you say, "The way of the Lord is not fair." House of Israel, I will judge every one of you after his ways.'" We can see in these verses that some may accuse God of being unfair, Ezekiel points out the impartial fair judgments of God. This is His creation. He will judge equitably and fairly. Damnation is the fault of the actions of the individual who committed the sin and failed to repent and turn to God. God is wholly innocent of the consequences taken by the individual because He created them with free will to choose their own direction. He provided His word, which attests to His nature, and He has been trying to call mankind back to Him since the time we fell away through sin.

Many people may struggle with Old Testament accounts of God destroying entire populations of people such as the worldwide flood (Genesis, chapter 6), the destruction of Sodom and Gomorrah (Genesis, chapter 19), or God's order to completely destroy the Canaanite cities by the armies of Israel (Deuteronomy, chapter 7). After all, how can we say "God is Love" when He orders the direct and complete destruction of entire populations of people?

This is a very good question and one that we must grapple with as Christians. In doing so, we must realize that while God is Love, He is also perfect in righteousness and justice. He is separate from sinners (and we are all sinners). We must remember the destruction of these populations were a direct result of their long defiance against God. God judged these populations of people because they had become too wicked to tolerate any further. Also, in the case of God's order to Israel to completely destroy the Canaanite cities, it was done with a higher purpose in mind:

> But of the cities of these peoples that Yahweh your God gives you for an inheritance, you shall save alive nothing that breathes; but you shall utterly destroy them: the Hittite, the Amorite, the Canaanite, the Perizzite, the Hivite, and the Jebusite, as Yahweh your God has commanded you; **that they not teach you to follow all their abominations, which they have done for their gods; so would you sin against Yahweh your God.** *[emphasis added]* ~ **Deuteronomy 20:16-18**

These Bible verses show that God had a higher purpose in mind, which required the complete destruction of these Canaanite populations. As God's chosen people, Israel was meant to be pure and holy. Israel was meant to serve as God's example to other people. As such, it was important that Israel not be led astray from worshiping the Lord. We must understand that God's judgment on these Canaanite communities was done as a direct result of their rebellion against Him over a very long period. God is a patient God, but He is also a perfectly just God. He will not tolerate sin indefinitely. It doesn't benefit us (as sinners) to think that we have a greater sense of justice than God. God alone has the responsibility to provide justice for a broken, wicked, and imperfect world. As a result, some of His judgments will appear to be unfair or harsh to us. But we don't have God's perspective or perfect vision. God's perfect justice is simply incomprehensible to us as mortal sinners. We must understand that a perfectly just God is blameless in these judgments. We should try to understand them, but only through the lens that God is perfectly just. As such, we should be careful when we attempt to judge God's actions.

The Bible makes it clear God showers both the righteous and the wicked with His blessings. We see evidence of this in the book of Matthew:

> . . . that you may be children of your Father who is in heaven. **For he makes his sun to rise on the evil and the good, and sends rain on the just and the unjust.** *[emphasis added]* For if you love those who love you, what reward do you have? Don't even the tax collectors do the same? If you only greet your friends, what more do you do than others? Don't even the tax collectors do

the same? Therefore you shall be perfect, just as your Father in heaven is perfect."~ *[emphasis added]* **Matthew 5:45-48**

The Bible also makes it clear God doesn't want the righteous to get caught up in the judgments He imposes upon the wicked. We can examine how God handled the destruction of Sodom and Gomorrah for evidence of this:

Yahweh said, "Will I hide from Abraham what I do, since Abraham will surely become a great and mighty nation, and all the nations of the earth will be blessed in him? For I have known him, to the end that he may command his children and his household after him, that they may keep the way of Yahweh, to do righteousness and justice; to the end that Yahweh may bring on Abraham that which he has spoken of him." Yahweh said, "Because the cry of Sodom and Gomorrah is great, and because their sin is very grievous, I will go down now, and see whether their deeds are as bad as the reports which have come to me. If not, I will know." The men turned from there, and went toward Sodom, but Abraham stood yet before Yahweh. Abraham came near, and said, "Will you consume the righteous with the wicked? What if there are fifty righteous within the city? Will you consume and not spare the place for the fifty righteous who are in it? May it be far from you to do things like that, to kill the righteous with the wicked, so that the righteous should be like the wicked. May that be far from you. Shouldn't the Judge of all the earth do right?" Yahweh said, "If I find in Sodom fifty righteous within the city, then I will spare the whole place for their sake." Abraham answered, "See now, I have taken it on myself to speak to the Lord, although I am dust and ashes. What if there will lack five of the fifty righteous? Will you destroy all the city for lack of five?" He said, "I will not destroy it if I find forty-five there." He spoke to him yet again, and said, "What if there are forty found there?" He said, "I will not do it for the forty's sake." He said, "Oh don't let the Lord be angry, and I will speak. What if there are thirty found there?" He said, "I will not do it if I find thirty there." He said, "See now, I have taken it on myself to speak to the Lord. What if there are twenty found there?" He said, "I will not destroy it for the twenty's sake." He said, "Oh

don't let the Lord be angry, and I will speak just once more. What if ten are found there?" He said, "I will not destroy it for the ten's sake." Yahweh went his way as soon as he had finished communing with Abraham, and Abraham returned to his place.
- **Genesis 18:16-33**

You can see from the above dialogue between Abraham and God that the Lord clearly says He would not destroy the cities of Sodom and Gomorrah if even ten righteous people were found in those cities. Its clear God makes a distinction between the righteous and the wicked in His judgments, and He would spare the wicked within an entire community of people if the righteous were amongst the wicked. God has the responsibility of providing justice to a broken world. These Bible verses show God acts with perfect justice. What sort of God would allow wickedness and evil to go unpunished? We may feel some of God's judgments on masses of humanity are unfair or heavy-handed, but we do not have God's perfect perspective. The Bible provides evidence that God's justice is perfect even if we can't completely comprehend it. We simply must trust in God's perfect justice and not question it using what limited perspective we might have.

GOD'S OMNISCIENT AND CONSISTENT NATURE

SOME MAY ASK HOW WE can be assured of God's omniscient and consistent nature when we profess to believe in both testaments of the Bible. These people argue these two testaments of the Bible are not consistent with each other: so how can they reflect consistency within God's nature?

My counter-argument is that the combined Old and New Testaments are a single contract between God and humanity. I would point out both testaments are completely consistent with each other. The Old Testament is looking for the appearance of the Messiah. It provides many prophecies of the Messiah and how He would be recognized. The New Testament provides accounts of the birth, life, crucifixion, and resurrection of Jesus, the Messiah. It shows that Jesus fulfilled all the prophecies contained within the Old Testament. Both documents are fully consistent with each other. God planned from the very beginning of creation how He would redeem humanity. He knew we would sin. He knew we would fall. Why wouldn't He? He can see the future as well as the past. The Bible states this clearly in Psalm 139:

> Yahweh, you have searched me, and you know me. You know my sitting down and my rising up. You perceive my thoughts from afar. You search out my path and my lying down, and are acquainted with all my ways. For there is not a word on my tongue, but, behold, Yahweh, you know it altogether. You hem me in behind and before. You laid your hand on me. This knowledge is beyond me. It's lofty. I can't attain it." ~ **Psalm 139:1-6**

There are many verses in the Bible that point out God's omniscience. Consider these two as examples:

> I declare the end from the beginning, and from ancient times things that are not yet done. I say: My counsel will stand, and I will do all that I please. ~ **Isaiah 46:10**

> In the beginning was the Word, and the Word was with God, and the Word was God. The same was in the beginning with God. All things were made through him. Without him, nothing was made that has been made. ~ **John 1:1-3**

The Bible declares God's word existed before time itself. God wrote the entire story of humanity before humanity ever existed. God also authored the most merciful and loving plan possible to save humanity after their fall. His plan is His story. His story has been playing out throughout history. His plan has never changed. His story is meant to bring the ultimate glory to God in the end. In the end all people of the earth will bow down and give glory to God (even people that don't currently believe in Him). God's purpose in bringing His word into being is to bring glory to Himself. We must not forget this as we play a role in His story. Knowing that God wrote the entire story of humanity before humanity ever existed, we can discern the following:

- The fall of mankind was foreknown by God.
- The crucifixion of Christ was foreordained by God as the price that would have to be paid for the atonement of all sin.

Given the Old and New Testaments of the Bible are completely consistent with each other, we can conclude that God's nature is also consistent. We can conclude that God is Omniscient and His nature is consistent.

Many people ask what God's plan was to save people who existed prior to revealing Jesus to them? After all, Jesus is said to be the single key to everyone's salvation, so how could the people that existed before Jesus be saved? To that I would say God says clearly that nature itself is enough to display the evidence of His existence.

> For the invisible things of him since the creation of the world are clearly seen, being perceived through the things that are made, even his everlasting power and divinity, **that they may be without excuse**. *[emphasis added]* ~ **Romans 1:20**

This verse makes it clear that the very creation speaks to God's existence. His eternal power and divinity have been clearly displayed in His creation. Therefore, mankind has no excuse for failing to honor and worship God even, without knowing of Jesus' existence. Furthermore, the Bible makes it clear righteousness was bestowed upon the patriarchs of the Bible for their faith. Jesus didn't exist at the time of the Biblical patriarchs. As a result, we can conclude that faith alone in God was enough to bestow righteousness upon people that existed prior to Jesus' existence.

MARK'S HAND

AGAIN, THIS IS A STORY as told to me from my mother's perspective, a story that I grew up with that resonated with me as an early Christian. The story speaks to God's ability to heal through the prayer of his followers.

When Mark came home from work one night, I could tell something was wrong. It turned out he had been involved in an accident at work. He was working at a General Motors assembly plant that was experiencing all sorts of labor disputes between the union workers and the management of the company. Mark's job as an assembly line supervisor was to make sure the assembly process ran as smoothly as possible. The labor dispute made his job extremely difficult. That night one of his workers shut down a conveyor belt to cause the seats to back up into each other. Mark realized what had happened and attempted to fix the problem by trying to re-start the conveyor. He braced his left hand on a conveyor belt and flipped the switch to re-start the assembly process. When the assembly process started, however, Mark could feel his left hand get sucked between the metal rollers of the conveyor belt. He quickly reached up and threw the switch to stop the assembly process but it was too late. The rollers came to a stop about three inches above his wrist. His hand was crushed between the rollers.

Mark said the pain was so severe he almost lost consciousness. Had he lost consciousness with his hand caught in the conveyor, he likely would have broken his hand at the wrist, but he was able to maintain consciousness despite the severe pain. Mark's workmates finally determined there were two options available to free his hand from the conveyor belt. The first option was to manually remove the rollers of the conveyor belt so Mark's hand could be released. This process would take a long time. The second option was to reverse the motor of the conveyor belt. Doing so would allow Mark's hand to be backed out from between the rollers. This option would be quicker but would be much more painful. Both options were presented to Mark, and he asked the workers to reverse the motor. He knew that waiting longer might cause him to lose consciousness and he was afraid of breaking his wrist. The employees reversed the motor, and the rollers reversed direction, releasing Mark's hand from the conveyor belt rollers.

Mark was seen within the medical department of the assembly plant, and they determined there weren't any broken bones, so he decided to continue working through the night. When Mark got home, I saw his hand for the first time. It was black and blue and resembled a large claw. Due to the large amount of swelling in the hand, it was difficult to see his fingers. His hand looked horrible. The next morning Mark decided to see a specialist. We waited for several hours in the waiting room without being seen, and Mark was in terrible pain. We had grown so tired of waiting we almost left the office. On our way out the door, however, the doctor met Mark. He took one look at Mark's hand and told him he needed to be admitted to the hospital right away. He was afraid Mark might have blood clots that could break free and possibly kill him. Once packed in ice, the medical staff examined the hand and determined there weren't any broken bones, but there was extensive soft tissue damage. The doctors feared they would need to perform skin graft surgery.

Mark and I had a friend who used to ride motorcycles. Our friend had been involved in a serious motorcycle accident and had required skin grafts over a good portion of his body. Mark and I were aware of the consequences of skin grafts. Our friend experienced frequent problems with his grafts. They were always cracking and bleeding, especially in colder weather. They also left ugly scars. I didn't want to see Mark have skin grafts, so I began to pray.

I always had a quiet corner in the house where I prayed. Mark's mother, Stella, told me how the old-time Nazarenes used to pray. They used to get down on their hands and knees and pray until they were sure they had an answer from God. I was still a new Christian, but I figured if this worked for them in the past, I was going to try it. I got down on my hands and knees and I prayed for hours. I asked God to heal Mark's hand, so he wouldn't require skin graft surgery. I told God it was okay, and I would understand if He decided not to heal Mark's hand completely, but I had to have an answer and wasn't going to get up from my hands and knees until I had His answer. After several hours of prayer, I received my answer. An awesome feeling came over me and a small voice said Mark's hand would be fine. I called Mark that night at the hospital and told him his hand would be fine and he wasn't going to require skin grafts.

The next morning Mark was scheduled for the skin graft surgery. I showed up at the hospital and there were many of Mark's friends there. I told them about my prayers and the answer Jesus provided me. One of

Mark's friends mocked me saying he talked to God also, and God had told him Mark was going to need skin grafts. I was undeterred, though, and remained 100 percent sure Mark wasn't going to require skin grafts. The doctors brought Mark down to the surgical suite and began to clean his hand to prepare it for surgery. To their amazement the skin tissue was regenerating on its own! The doctor informed Mark he would need to remain in the hospital for quite some time, but it didn't appear skin grafts would be required!

Mark spent about seventeen days in the hospital with his hand immobilized in an elevated sling. His hand was iced continuously throughout his hospital stay. If you were to look at Mark's hand today you would never know it had been crushed. He has full use of both hands and his left hand shows no sign of injury. In addition, Mark has very little pain in his left hand. He has much more arthritic pain in his right hand than he does in his left. I believe when Jesus healed Mark's left hand, he made it better than it ever was. I believe Jesus cured everything that had ever been wrong with Mark's left hand. Once again, God showed what a caring and loving God He is. God's answer to prayer was miraculous, timely, and awesome!

I found out later there was a safety mechanism on this conveyor belt that failed at the time of Mark's hand being stuck in the conveyor belt. The safety mechanism was designed to expand and pop the second roller out if any object got caught in the conveyor belt. The failure of this safety mechanism allowed Mark's hand to be crushed. When employees were determining their options for freeing Mark's hand, they mysteriously overlooked one of the most obvious options. There was a button designed to release the conveyor belt in this type of incident. None of Mark's coworkers were aware of this option. I learned there had been two other similar incidents of this nature reported. The safety button release mechanism had been attempted in each of those incidents and failed. In both incidents the safety release mechanism caused a piece of the conveyor belt system to drop down, severing each employee's hand. In Mark's case his fellow employees mysteriously failed to realize this was even an option available to them. I believe God was looking after Mark. He allowed Mark to remain conscious and provided him with the answer that would free his hand from the machinery and cause him the least amount of damage.

Matthew 4:23-25 says the following:

> Jesus went throughout Galilee, teaching in their synagogues, preaching the good news of the kingdom, and healing every disease and sickness among the people. News about Him spread all over Syria, and people brought to Him all who were ill with various diseases, those suffering severe pain, the demon possessed, the epileptics, and the paralytics, and He healed them. Large crowds from Galilee, the Decapolis, Jerusalem, Judea, and the region across the Jordan followed Him.

This verse meant a lot to me as I was praying for Mark's hand to be healed. There is no doubt in my mind Mark's hand was protected by the Holy Spirit when he got his hand caught between the rollers of the conveyor belt. There is no doubt in my mind Mark's hand was healed through the power of prayer.

PROPHECIES CONCERNING JESUS' LIFE, MINISTRY, AND CRUCIFIXION

MY LIFE HAS BEEN TOUCHED in so many ways by the direct hand of God. I have shared a few moments of my life with you in this book so you may know there is a God and He is still in the active business of performing miracles today. He is at work in the world today and He still answers prayers for those who believe in Him. One of the reasons I believe in God is simply because I have felt his direct presence in my life. It's hard to disbelieve when you have felt and witnessed God in a very personal way. In addition to having felt God's direct presence in my life my faith has been bolstered in understanding there are numerous prophesies that have been fulfilled in the Bible concerning Jesus' life, death, and resurrection. The Old Testament of the Bible contains many prophecies about Jesus' life and the New Testament of the Bible contains the written account of the fulfillment of those prophecies in stunning detail. God's word existed before His creation, so it shouldn't surprise us that His word contains many prophetic accounts of Jesus' life.

It is the very existence of the Old Testament of the Bible that provides the basis for the proof that Jesus is who he claimed to be – your savior and the son of God. The Old Testament is a book of historical facts, not myths. The Old Testament was written over the course of many centuries. The book was completed long before Jesus was born, and yet the authors of the Old Testament documented his life in explicit detail. The book contains incredible prophesies about every aspect of the ministry of Jesus. These prophecies were written by different authors in different periods of history yet when pieced together they establish an unmistakable depiction of the ministry of Jesus exactly as it unfolded. It is a true miracle that this collection of different authors within different historical contexts could have produced such a complete and astoundingly accurate picture of Jesus. This proves that while there were many men who helped write the Old Testament, the book itself was authored by the hand of God. The following are samples of the prophecies and foreshadowing events included in the Old Testament centering around the ministry of Jesus along with the written account of their fulfillment in the New Testament.

IN THE OLD TESTAMENT:	IN THE NEW TESTAMENT:
The voice of one who calls out, "Prepare the way of Yahweh in the wilderness! Make a level highway in the desert for our God. ~ **Isaiah 40:3**	In those days, John the Baptizer came, preaching in the wilderness of Judea, saying, "Repent, for the Kingdom of Heaven is at hand!" For this is he who was spoken of by Isaiah the prophet, saying, "The voice of one crying in the wilderness, make the way of the Lord ready! Make his paths straight!" ~ **Matthew 3:1-3**
He said, "Listen now, house of David. Is it not enough for you to try the patience of men, that you will try the patience of my God also? Therefore the Lord himself will give you a sign. Behold, the virgin will conceive, and bear a son, and shall call his name Immanuel." ~ **Isaiah 7:13-14**	Behold, the virgin shall be with child, and shall give birth to a son. They shall call his name Immanuel," which is, being interpreted, "God with us." ~ **Matthew 1:23**
Who has believed our message? To whom has Yahweh's arm been revealed? For he grew up before him as a tender plant, and as a root out of dry ground. He has no good looks or majesty. When we see him, there is no beauty that we should desire him. He was despised and rejected by men, a man of suffering and acquainted with disease. He was despised as one from whom men hide their face; and we didn't respect him. Surely he has borne our sickness and carried our suffering; yet we considered him plagued, struck by God, and afflicted. But he was pierced for our transgressions. He was crushed for our iniquities. The punishment that brought our peace was on him; and by his wounds we are healed. All we like sheep have gone astray. Everyone has turned to his own way; and Yahweh has laid on him the iniquity of us all.	This set of Bible verses from Isaiah paint a vivid description of Jesus and point out that He would take on our many transgressions upon himself. Isaiah points out that Jesus would be pierced for our transgressions – exactly as it unfolded in His crucifixion. Further, these verses indicate that Jesus would not open His mouth to speak in His defense, but He would go willingly to His death on the cross. All this is confirmed in the gospel accounts of Jesus' death.

He was oppressed, yet when he was afflicted, he didn't open his mouth. As a lamb that is led to the slaughter, and as a sheep that before its shearers is silent, so he didn't open his mouth. He was taken away by oppression and judgment. As for his generation, who considered that he was cut off out of the land of the living and stricken for the disobedience of my people? They made his grave with the wicked, and with a rich man in his death, although he had done no violence, nor was any deceit in his mouth. Yet it pleased Yahweh to bruise him. He has caused him to suffer. When you make his soul an offering for sin, he will see his offspring. He will prolong his days and Yahweh's pleasure will prosper in his hand. After the suffering of his soul, he will see the light and be satisfied. My righteous servant will justify many by the knowledge of himself; and he will bear their iniquities. Therefore I will give him a portion with the great. He will divide the plunder with the strong; because he poured out his soul to death and was counted with the transgressors.

Yet he bore the sins of many and made intercession for the transgressors. ~ **Isaiah chapter 53**

I will open my mouth in a parable. I will utter dark sayings of old. ~ **Psalm 78:2**	Jesus taught in parables, and there are many accounts of the parables that Jesus taught contained within the pages of the New Testament of the Bible.

But you, Bethlehem Ephrathah, being small among the clans of Judah, out of you one will come out to me that is to be ruler in Israel; whose goings out are from of old, from ancient times.	Now when Jesus was born in Bethlehem of Judea in the days of King Herod, behold, wise men from the east came to Jerusalem, saying, "Where is he who is born King of the Jews? For we saw his star in the east and have come to worship him." ~ **Matthew 2:1-2**

Therefore he will abandon them until the time that she who is in labor gives birth. Then the rest of his brothers will return to the children of Israel. He shall stand, and shall shepherd in the strength of Yahweh, in the majesty of the name of Yahweh his God: and they will live, for then he will be great to the ends of the earth. ~ **Micah 5:2-4**

When the angels went away from them into the sky, the shepherds said to one another, "Let's go to Bethlehem, now, and see this thing that has happened, which the Lord has made known to us." ~ **Luke 2:15**

Rejoice greatly, daughter of Zion! Shout, daughter of Jerusalem! Behold, your King comes to you! He is righteous, and having salvation; lowly, and riding on a donkey, even on a colt, the foal of a donkey. ~ **Zechariah 9:9**

When they came near to Jerusalem and came to Bethpage, to the Mount of Olives, then Jesus sent two disciples, saying to them, "Go into the village that is opposite you, and immediately you will find a donkey tied, and a colt with her. Untie them and bring them to me. If anyone says anything to you, you shall say, 'The Lord needs them,' and immediately he will send them." All this was done that it might be fulfilled which was spoken through the prophet, saying, "Tell the daughter of Zion, behold, your King comes to you, humble, and riding on a donkey, on a colt, the foal of a donkey." The disciples went and did just as Jesus commanded them and brought the donkey and the colt and laid their clothes on them; and he sat on them. A very great multitude spread their clothes on the road. Others cut branches from the trees and spread them on the road. The multitudes who went in front of him, and those who followed, kept shouting, "Hosanna to the son of David! Blessed is he who comes in the name of the Lord! Hosanna in the highest!" ~ **Matthew 21:1-9**

Yes, my own familiar friend, in whom I trusted, who ate bread with me, has lifted up his heel against me. ~ **Psalm 41:9**

I am not referring to all of you; I know those I have chosen. But this is to fulfill this passage of Scripture: He who shared my bread has turned against me.' 'I am telling you now before it happens, so that when it does happen you will believe that I am who I am. ~ **John 13:18-19**

I said to them, "If you think it best, give me my wages; and if not, keep them." So they weighed for my wages thirty pieces of silver. Yahweh said to me, "Throw it to the potter, the handsome price that I was valued at by them!" I took the thirty pieces of silver, and threw them to the potter, in Yahweh's house. ~ **Zechariah 11:12-13**

and [he] said, what are you willing to give me if I deliver him to you?" So, they weighed out for him thirty pieces of silver. From that time he sought opportunity to betray him. ~ **Matthew 26: 15-16**

Then Judas, who betrayed him, when he saw that Jesus was condemned, felt remorse, and brought back the thirty pieces of silver to the chief priests and elders, saying, "I have sinned in that I betrayed innocent blood.' But they said, "What is that to us? You see to it." He threw down the pieces of silver in the sanctuary and departed. Then he went away and hanged himself. The chief priests took the pieces of silver and said, "It's not lawful to put them into the treasury, since it is the price of blood." They took counsel, and bought the potter's field with them to bury strangers in. Therefore that field has been called "The Field of Blood" to this day. Then that which was spoken through Jeremiah the prophet was fulfilled, saying, "They took the thirty pieces of silver, the price of him upon whom a price had been set, whom some of the children of Israel priced, and they gave them for the potter's field, as the Lord commanded me.'" ~ **Matthew 27: 3-10**

(This set of Bible verses speaks of the betrayal of Judas Iscariot who betrayed Jesus and how the blood money would be used to purchase the potter's field.)

For dogs have surrounded me. A company of evildoers have enclosed me. They have pierced my hands and feet. ~ **Psalm 22:16**	This verse describes the method of crucifixion as Jesus' hands and feet were pierced when they hung Him on the cross.
They divide my garments among them. They cast lots for my clothing. ~ **Psalm 22:18**	When they had crucified him, they divided his clothing among them, casting lots. ~ **Matthew 27:35**
They also gave me poison for my food. In my thirst, they gave me vinegar to drink. ~ **Psalm 69:21**	They gave him sour wine to drink mixed with gall. When he had tasted it, he would not drink. ~ **Matthew 27:34**

All those who see me mock me. They insult me with their lips. They shake their heads, saying, "He trusts in Yahweh. Let him deliver him. Let him rescue him, since he delights in him." **Psalm 22:7-8**	Matthew 27:27-44 Describes the mocking in great detail.

He protects all of his bones. Not one of them is broken." ~ **Psalm 34:20** -and- and they will look to me whom they have pierced; and they shall mourn for him, as one mourns for his only son, and will grieve bitterly for him, as one grieves for his firstborn. ~ **Zechariah 12:10**	However, one of the soldiers pierced his side with a spear, and immediately blood and water came out. He who has seen has testified, and his testimony is true. He knows that he tells the truth, that you may believe. For these things happened that the Scripture might be fulfilled, "A bone of him will not be broken." Again, another Scripture says, "They will look on him whom they pierced." ~ **John 19: 34-37**

At the ninth hour Jesus cried out with a loud voice, saying, "Eloi, Eloi, lama sabachthani?" which is, being interpreted, means, "My God, my God, why have you forsaken me?" ~ **Mark 15:34.** Jesus' declaration on the cross when He says "My God, My God, why have you forsaken me" points to Psalm 22. This Psalm should be read in its entirety to understand the full context of what Jesus was saying on the cross, but many scholars believe that Jesus spoke those words to point people to Psalm 22 as it is a direct prophecy in the Old Testament that described Jesus' death on the cross in full detail.

> My God, my God, why have you forsaken me? Why are you so far from helping me, and from the words of my groaning? My God, I cry in the daytime, but you don't answer; in the night season and am not silent. But you are holy, you who inhabit the praises of Israel. Our fathers trusted in you. They trusted, and you delivered them. They cried to you, and were delivered. They trusted in you and were not disappointed. But I am a worm, and no man; a reproach of men, and despised by the people. All those who see me mock me. They insult me with their lips. They shake their heads, saying, "He trusts in Yahweh. Let him deliver him. Let him rescue him, since he delights in him." But

you brought me out of the womb. You made me trust while at my mother's breasts. I was thrown on you from my mother's womb. You are my God since my mother bore me. Don't be far from me, for trouble is near. For there is no one to help. Many bulls have surrounded me. Strong bulls of Bashan have encircled me. They open their mouths wide against me, lions tearing prey and roaring. I am poured out like water. All my bones are out of joint. My heart is like wax. It is melted within me. My strength is dried up like a potsherd. My tongue sticks to the roof of my mouth. You have brought me into the dust of death. For dogs have surrounded me. A company of evildoers have enclosed me. They have pierced my hands and feet. I can count all of my bones. They look and stare at me. They divide my garments among them. They cast lots for my clothing. But don't be far off, Yahweh. You are my help. Hurry to help me! Deliver my soul from the sword, my precious life from the power of the dog. Save me from the lion's mouth! Yes, you have rescued me from the horns of the wild oxen. I will declare your name to my brothers. Among the assembly, I will praise you. You who fear Yahweh, praise him! All you descendants of Jacob, glorify him! Stand in awe of him, all you descendants of Israel! For he has not despised nor abhorred the affliction of the afflicted, neither has he hidden his face from him; but when he cried to him, he heard. My praise of you comes in the great assembly. I will pay my vows before those who fear him. The humble shall eat and be satisfied. They shall praise Yahweh who seek after him. Let your hearts live forever. All the ends of the earth shall remember and turn to Yahweh. All the relatives of the nations shall worship before you. For the kingdom is Yahweh's. He is the ruler over the nations. All the rich ones of the earth shall eat and worship. All those who go down to the dust shall bow before him, even he who can't keep his soul alive. Posterity shall serve him. Future generations shall be told about the Lord. They shall come and shall declare his righteousness to a people that shall be born, for he has done it. ~**Psalms chapter 22**

The pages of the Old Testament describe the entire ministry of Jesus, yet the period between the writing of the Old Testament and New Testament is about 400 years. How can a book dating 400 years prior to the start of the New Testament foretell just about every event in the ministry of Jesus? Surely God is author!

These prophesies, when taken together, are clearly attributed to only one man in history. It has been argued that Jesus could have fulfilled the prophesies foretold in the Old Testament simply because He knew them beforehand, that Jesus could have caused events to happen to make it appear He was the promised messiah. While it's true Jesus knew the prophesies of the Old Testament very well, it would have been impossible for any man to have arranged the fulfillment of many of those prophesies. For instance, how could Jesus make sure John the Baptist was there to prepare the way for Him? How could Jesus make sure He was born in the house of David by a virgin? How could Jesus set the payment amount for his betrayal at thirty pieces of silver? How could He control how the Jewish authority used the blood money to purchase the Potter's field? For that matter, how could Jesus select the method of his death? He certainly hadn't done anything to deserve crucifixion and yet that was the method of execution declared for Him. The fact of the matter is the Old Testament contains many prophecies about Jesus that were fulfilled and documented within the pages of the New Testament. This is why you can have faith in Jesus as your savior.

FAITH, HOPE, AND LOVE

"But now faith, hope, and love remain—these three. The greatest of these is love." ~ 1 **Corinthians 13:13**

DO YOU KNOW WHY LOVE is called out to be the greatest? Love is the greatest simply because God tells us in the Bible: He is love. We are to set nothing above God. Faith represents the testimony of the apostles and all true believers of Jesus. No matter what the world tries to do to them, their testimony survives. Those martyred are the greatest witness to the gospel. They were willing to die rather than tell a lie. They allowed themselves to be martyred. They laid their life down willingly for the message of the gospel. They died for what they knew, beyond a shadow of a doubt, was true. How many people would choose to die for something they aren't sure they believe in? I say nobody would make that choice. But these true believers freely laid their life down rather than give another (false) testimony. That's because they knew they carried the one true message the world needed to hear for its salvation and reconciliation to God, and they were willing to die for that message.

Hope can be seen in the representation of Israel. Israel's relationship with God impacted how strong they were able to become. Under King David's reign Israel was devoted to God. They became a great nation. Israel greatly expanded their boundaries under King David. They were able to capture the city of Jerusalem. At the beginning of King Solomon's reign Israel became an even greater nation. Under King Solomon's early reign, they were able to build God's temple. They expanded the nation's boundaries even further. Later in King Solomon's reign Israel started to fall into idolatry. They were lead down the path of idolatry because Solomon's many wives lead him into worshiping and building temples to other gods. Because Solomon allowed idolatry to enter Israel they were punished at the hands of God. Ultimately, Israel was shaken to its core when ten of twelve tribes fell to the Assyrians. Yet, through all these things, at least some remnant of Israel's population remained. Israel endured, in some part, as a population throughout history. The Jewish population has never ceased to exist. Even in their destruction there remained a remnant of their population that God protected. Even when there was no sovereign nation of Israel the Jewish population never ceased to exist. There was no sovereign nation of Israel between 135AD and 1947 and yet, despite that fact, the Jewish population never ceased to exist. This is simply amazing and provides evidence of God's divine protection over the population of Israel. Further, Israel's rebirth as a sovereign nation in 1947 provides further evidence of God's providence over Israel. It is truly amazing that Israel was able to become a sovereign nation again in modern times. God chose Israel as His chosen people. God didn't choose Israel because they were any more righteous than any other population on earth. God chose Israel simply as His display of grace toward them. He chose to use Israel as an example to all people. Our role in the story is to simply allow God to use us as His tool (His hands and feet to spread His word). The Bible verse that comes to mind is Psalm 46:10 "Be still and know that I am God. I will be exalted among the nations. I will be exalted in the earth."

For those reading this book, I pray for your personal salvation. God blesses you with a unique purpose in His story. If you chose to accept God's offer of salvation, I would challenge you to use your free will to find out what your God-given purpose is. Listen for the whisper. Very seldom does God present Himself through fire, anger, and rage. Elijah serves as an example of how God speaks to us. Understand God speaks to those who choose to follow Him in a whisper most of the time. Very seldom does God chose to speak in a loud voice. 1 Kings 19:9-18 teaches us that God's presence is not found in a great wind, nor an earthquake, nor a firestorm, but rather in a still, small voice." (verse 12) God is love. Trust in Him and listen to the whisper presented to you by the Holy Spirit.

FLOWERS FOR THE PASTOR'S WIFE

I WANT TO SHARE WITH you a story my mother shared with me during my early Christian walk. This story provides an example of how we, as Christians, are sometimes led by the Holy Spirit to do things that don't make any sense to us at the time, but if we follow those prompts of the Holy Spirit sometimes, they lead to miraculous results, and we are richly blessed by following and acting upon those prompts we receive as His followers.

I was very active as the youth leader for the teens at the church Mark and I considered to be our home church for quite a few years. I grew to dearly love the church but for various reasons Mark and I felt we needed to leave the church for a period. While attending other churches we always kept tabs on our home church. One day, when I was working as the youth director of a different church, I had an unmistakable call from the Holy Spirt to return to my home church. Obedient to God's call, Mark and I attended a service the next Sunday. During that service the pastor announced he felt called to leave the church because God was leading his life in a different direction. His announcement surprised Mark and me, and we both felt there was a reason God led us back to our home church. We didn't know if it had anything to do with this pastor's announcement, but God's leading was unmistakable. I felt I needed to be obedient, so Mark and I remained at our home church.

Both Mark and I were happy to be back in our home church. I wasn't actively serving in the church, but I was attending the services on a regular basis. At this time in my life, I wasn't working outside of the home. I really wanted to spend all the time I possibly could with my twins (Tami and Tom) before they started attending school on a full-time basis. Mark and I made the decision we were going to live on a single income to allow this to happen. We had to watch our money a bit, but we always seemed to have enough. We tithed regularly, and I watched as God provided for all our needs. Money was tight, but we always had enough to do whatever we wanted.

One morning as I was driving my car, I suddenly sensed the Holy Spirit directing me to buy a bouquet of flowers and take them to the pastor's wife. I started to argue with God in my mind. I told Him I thought the request was crazy. I told Him I barely knew the new pastor or his wife. I couldn't just go to their house with a bouquet of flowers. I told Him they would think I was crazy. I also told Him I didn't have any money to buy the flowers. I didn't have a credit card, so it wasn't like I could just charge the bouquet of flowers. This argument went back and forth in my mind for quite some time. Finally, I drove past a florist, and I told God, "Fine, I'll go into that florist shop, and I will buy whatever bouquet of flowers I can buy with the money I have in my wallet." I didn't have that much money, and I remember thinking to myself as I entered the florist shop this was crazy. I told the Lord I wasn't going to be able to buy flowers with the amount of money I had in my wallet.

As I entered the shop, however, I noticed the florist was having a sale on daisies. I found I had exactly the correct amount of money in my wallet to purchase a bouquet of daisies (down to the penny). I purchased a bouquet of daisies and left the florist shop. While I was on my way to the pastor's house, I continued to argue with God in my mind. I kept telling myself this was crazy. I kept telling myself I didn't even know these people, and this was going to seem crazy to them.

By the time I got to the pastor's house I had been arguing back and forth my mind for quite some time. I walked to the pastor's front door and knocked. The pastor answered and I told him he didn't know me, but I attended his services on a regular basis. I told him I purchased a bouquet of flowers for his wife. I told him this was going to sound crazy, but I felt led by God to buy these flowers and give them to his wife.

The pastor looked at me and told me I needed to give the flowers to his wife. He told me this was very important. I found the pastor's wife in the study of their home. When I gave the flowers to his wife she started to cry. She was crying quite a bit, so I thought I had done something wrong. I started to apologize to her for bringing the flowers to her. She stopped me from apologizing. She told me they felt God was leading them in a different direction in their lives. She said she wanted to be sure she was doing the right thing, so she had asked for wisdom. She asked God for an unmistakable sign from Him so she would know what they were supposed to do. She told me she had asked God to provide a bouquet of daisies as a sign He was leading their lives in a different direction!

James 1:5-8 says the following:

> "If any of you lacks wisdom, he should ask God, who gives gen-
> erously to all without finding fault, and it will be given to him.
> But when he asks, he must believe and not doubt, because he
> who doubts is like a wave of the sea, blown and tossed by the
> wind. That man should not think he will receive anything from
> the Lord; he is a double-minded man, unstable in all he does."

The scripture makes it clear we, as Christians, have a right to ask for wisdom from our heavenly Father. He tells us He will grant wisdom to His followers, but we must have complete faith in the Lord. We cannot doubt He will provide wisdom when we ask for it. In this case, the pastor's wife asked for wisdom from the Lord. The Lord answered her prayer in an unmistakable manner. I think it is truly amazing I was fortunate enough to carry God's message to the pastor's wife. I was fortunate enough to be the bearer of the daisies! I was truly blessed by this experience. I argued with God about doing this task the entire time I was performing it. It wasn't until I completely performed the task for God I realized why He had asked me to do this.

It's important to be obedient to God's calling. If we feel unmistakably God is leading us in a direction, no matter how trivial or crazy it might seem, we need to follow His calling. It would have been very easy to say this was all just a crazy thought that had entered my mind. I could've very easily ignored this thought and gone on with the normal course of my day. I was obedient to the calling, however, and I was truly blessed by this experience.

THE LIVES AND TESTIMONY OF THE EARLY APOSTLES

THE EARLY APOSTLES HAD NO selfish motives. From a worldly perspective, they had nothing to gain and much to lose by spreading the message of the resurrection of Jesus. The apostles were men of utmost character, chosen by the hand of God. The early apostles lived simple lives. They didn't get rich or attain any profit from spreading their message. Furthermore, they endured great ridicule and persecution. Virtually all the apostles were martyred and suffered horrible deaths. Through all this persecution, and with very little worldly wealth to gain, they never renounced their faith in the message they were spreading. This message is documented in the New Testament of the Bible. If you believe in no other non-fiction book, you should believe the New Testament of the Bible because the authors of the New Testament paid a heavy price to bring the message to you. Look at Paul's life as an example. Acts 7:54-59 tells us Paul, as Saul, was totally devoted to the Jewish faith. He was present at the stoning of Stephen. He even looked after their coats while the stoning took place. Paul, as Saul, persecuted and killed Christians. After Jesus revealed himself to Saul, however, he became completely devoted to spreading the Christian message. Here is Paul's own account of his conversion, and the response of those who heard his story:

> "Brothers and fathers, listen to the defense which I now make to you." When they heard that he spoke to them in the Hebrew language, they were even more quiet. He said, "I am indeed a Jew, born in Tarsus of Cilicia, but brought up in this city at the feet of Gamaliel, instructed according to the strict tradition of the law of our fathers, being zealous for God, even as you all are today. I persecuted this Way to the death, binding and delivering into prisons both men and women, as also the high priest and all the council of the elders testify, from whom also I received letters to the brothers, and traveled to Damascus to bring them also who were there to Jerusalem in bonds to be punished. As I made my journey, and came close to Damascus, about noon, suddenly a great light shone around me from the sky. I fell to the ground,

and heard a voice saying to me, 'Saul, Saul, why are you perse-
cuting me?' I answered, 'Who are you, Lord?' He said to me, 'I
am Jesus of Nazareth, whom you persecute.' "Those who were
with me indeed saw the light and were afraid, but they didn't understand the voice of him who spoke to me. I said, 'What shall
I do, Lord?' The Lord said to me, 'Arise, and go into Damascus.
There you will be told about all the things which are appointed
for you to do.' When I couldn't see for the glory of that light,
being led by the hand of those who were with me, I came into
Damascus. One Ananias, a devout man according to the law,
well reported of by all the Jews who lived in Damascus, came
to me, and standing by me said to me, 'Brother Saul, receive
your sight!' In that very hour I looked up at him. He said, 'The
God of our fathers has appointed you to know his will, and to
see the Righteous One, and to hear a voice from his mouth. For
you will be a witness for him to all men of what you have seen
and heard. Now why do you wait? Arise, be baptized, and wash
away your sins, calling on the name of the Lord.' "When I had
returned to Jerusalem, and while I prayed in the temple, I fell
into a trance, and saw him saying to me, 'Hurry and get out of
Jerusalem quickly, because they will not receive testimony concerning me from you.' I said, 'Lord, they themselves know that
I imprisoned and beat in every synagogue those who believed
in you. When the blood of Stephen, your witness, was shed, I
also was standing by, consenting to his death, and guarding the
cloaks of those who killed him.' "He said to me, 'Depart, for I
will send you out far from here to the Gentiles.'" They listened
to him until he said that; then they lifted up their voice and
said, "Rid the earth of this fellow, for he isn't fit to live!" As they
cried out, threw off their cloaks, and threw dust into the air, the
commanding officer commanded him to be brought into the
barracks, ordering him to be examined by scourging, that he
might know for what crime they shouted against him like that."
~ **Acts 22:1-24**

Paul endured terrible things as he spread the message of Jesus. He
was stoned to the point people thought he was dead. Acts 14: 19,20
provide an account of this stoning when it says, "But some Jews from

Antioch and Iconium came there, and having persuaded the multitudes, they stoned Paul, and dragged him out of the city, supposing that he was dead. But as the disciples stood around him, he rose up, and entered into the city. On the next day he went out with Barnabas to Derbe."

Paul was shipwrecked three times, arrested numerous times, and stoned to the point people thought he was dead. How many other people facing such persecution and setbacks would wonder if God was really with them? Paul never doubted his purpose. He knew once he had come face to face with Jesus on the road to Damascus his one purpose in life was to spread the message of the gospel. He carried out this purpose no matter what obstacles stood in his path. That's true conviction! The fact is Paul had a life-changing event on the road to Damascus, one that turned his entire life toward spreading the gospel no matter the personal cost. One brief encounter with Jesus on the road to Damascus completely changed Paul's life. Paul was ultimately put in prison and martyred for spreading this message. Only one thing can explain this – Paul's encounter with Jesus made him believe, beyond a shadow of a doubt, Jesus was the promised messiah that had been, up to that point, rejected by the Jews.

Besides Paul, all the other early apostles also faced severe persecution for spreading the message of the gospel. Peter faced terrible persecution and imprisonment. Ultimately Peter was executed (tradition says he was crucified upside down) for his beliefs. Peter is the same apostle that denied knowing Jesus three times prior to Jesus' death. (Luke 22:54-62) After Jesus died on the cross, was resurrected from the dead, and had reappeared to His apostles, Peter had a renewed conviction to spread the message of Jesus. Peter went to the grave and never again renounced Jesus. He lived with Jesus, saw miracles Jesus performed, and was visited by the Holy Spirit. If Peter ever doubted Jesus was the savior, he certainly had plenty of motivation and time to renounce his beliefs. Peter never did. Instead, he faced ridicule, imprisonment, and persecution. He endured a horrible death as a martyr. Peter continued to spread the message of Jesus. There is no stronger evidence that Jesus is who He claimed to be than the life story of his earliest apostles. The testimony of the earliest apostles is enough evidence for me to believe, and I pray your heart is also opened enough to hear the message the early apostles were sharing with the world.

THE NEED FOR A SAVIOR

GOD CREATED ADAM AND EVE with freedom of choice and gave them responsibilities they were to fulfill within the Garden of Eden. They were to be active participants in God's divine plan of creation. God created them in His image. They were to reflect God's divine and holy nature. God tasked Adam and Eve with the responsibility to work and care for the Garden of Eden. They were to reside in paradise, but they weren't simply to relax. They had specific responsibilities to nurture and care for the garden. They were to have dominion over all of God's creation. Beyond these responsibilities, God very clearly forbid them from eating from the tree of knowledge. Genesis 2:17 says, "but you shall not eat of the tree of the knowledge of good and evil; for in the day that you eat of it, you will surely die."

Through Satan's temptation and deception Adam and Eve made the conscious decision to defy God's command. As soon as they ate from the tree of knowledge, they committed all of mankind to a death sentence. The need for a savior was born at that very moment. Before that point in time Adam and Eve never knew what sin was. Eating from the tree of knowledge provided Adam and Eve with the knowledge of good and evil. It is through the combination of free will and the knowledge of good and evil they were open to sin. When they ate from the tree of knowledge, they were also provided the ability to feel pride and shame. This is why Adam and Eve realized they were naked. The knowledge of the importance of self (self-centered thought) corrupted the very nature of God's creation. This is the reason so many marriages struggle and fail. Most marriages are destroyed by an unwillingness to compromise between partners. Prior to receiving knowledge of your own self-importance, you would naturally want to compromise. You would naturally want to fulfill the desires of your partner. This is why eating from the tree of knowledge became such a disaster for humanity. It affected our relationship with God as well as our relationship with each other.

Adam and Eve's defiance against God's command created the problem of sin within the Garden of Eden that ultimately needed a resolution. God alone has the power to solve the problem of sin against Him. God's ultimate plan for solving the problem of sin is through the shed blood of Jesus Christ. Within the garden of Eden God replaced Adam and Eve's cloths with the skin of an animal. The required death (sacrifice) of an animal to clothe Adam and Eve can be viewed as a foreshadowing event of the blood sacrifices that are documented within the Old Testament. This is the first act in the Bible of covering sin with the shed blood of an animal, and it was God that would make this first blood sacrifice on behalf of Adam and Eve.

Within the pages of the Old Testament God lays out the rules for sacrifice that would atone for sin. The rules of sacrificial atonement made it clear a blood sacrifice was required. Further, it required a perfect animal from the flock to be selected for the sacrifice to be acceptable to God—an animal with any defect was not acceptable to God. People were to bring an animal that represented the best of their flock for their sacrificial atonement. Likewise, in the New Testament of the Bible God provided perfection from His flock in the form of Jesus Christ for the sacrificial atonement of our sins. The pages of the Old Testament provide the account of Abraham's sacrifice of his son Isaac as a parallel to the sacrifice God would ultimately provide in His son Jesus for the atonement of all sin. Abraham's offering of his son Isaac is described in Genesis chapter 22. Abraham's willingness to sacrifice his son Isaac within the pages of the Old Testament foreshadow God's willingness to sacrifice His son for us in the New Testament. The sacrificial rules within the pages of the Old Testament were not sufficient to solve the problem of sin once and for all. That required the perfect sacrifice of God's own son. God willingly offered His son on the cross for us as Abraham was willing to offer Isaac as a sacrifice when he was being tested by God. Ultimately, God made the most merciful option available to us to obtain our salvation. Jesus' sacrifice for the atonement of sin is the only thing that pardons us from that death sentence and allows us to enter a relationship with a perfect God. The gift of eternal life will be bestowed upon those whose names are written in the lamb's book of life. This reward will be bestowed upon us at His second coming, as part of the final judgment of mankind. The gift of eternal life will be bestowed upon true believers as a reward for staying faithful to Him.

The gift of salvation offered through the sacrifice Jesus made on the cross for the atonement of your sins is a truly merciful act by a loving God. The sacrifice on the cross is the only thing that allows God's pardon, once and for all, for your sins. We took a death sentence upon ourselves when we took a bite from the fruit of the tree of knowledge in the Garden of Eden, but God offers the gift of salvation to us so that we may come into an everlasting presence with our Lord.

> But may the God of all grace, who called you to his eternal glory
> by Christ Jesus, after you have suffered a little while, perfect,
> establish, strengthen, and settle you. ~ **1 Peter 5:10**

This Bible verse states you will be required to suffer for a little while, but eternal grace is offered to those who believe in Him. God orchestrated everything (all of creation) to march down the path to this conclusion. For those who have endured a moment of suffering they will eventually be rewarded with eternal life. Once awarded eternal life, they will worship and honor God in what will be a new creation as God remakes the entire universe to allow us to reside together for eternity.

FREEDOM OF CHOICE

GOD GAVE MANKIND FREE WILL to choose their own destiny. You can choose to believe in the existence of God, or you can choose to be an atheist. God doesn't want people to live with Him in eternity because they were forced to do so. He provided us with free will to enable a choice. We get to heaven through believing the only way our sins can be covered is through the perfect blood of Jesus shed on the cross. The Bible is clear: we will be *rewarded* based upon our works, but we *get to heaven* through His grace of salvation. My fear for people who reject God's gift of salvation is they will hear these words when facing Jesus upon His second coming, "I never knew you. Away from Me, you evildoers!" (Matthew 7:23)

God endows everyone with free will. We have a choice to believe in Him or not. The atheist would say there is no God. They would tell you science will eventually answer all of mankind's questions. One of the reasons I choose to believe in God is because, from my experience, complex things have been designed by intelligence. When we look at complex objects like a car, plane, or bike we know someone with intelligence designed all the parts to work together to perform a specific function. Each part serves a specific purpose. The person who created the object figured out how all the different parts should fit together to perform specific functions to make the object they created work the way they intended it to. I see many complex things in nature as well. Human beings have fingers, toes, eyes, and ears. All those parts work together to perform specific functions. I think to myself, am I supposed to believe all this complexity just happened at random, completely by chance?

The atheist argues that a bunch of atoms, molecules, and substances got struck by lightning at some point in our distant past. Over the course of billions of years all those substances somehow randomly formed a single cell organism. The single cell organism figured out how to replicate itself. Once enough single-celled organisms figured out how to replicate themselves, they figured out how to combine themselves to make the first multi-cell organism. That first multi-cell organism then figured out how to replicate itself and once there were enough multi-cell organisms, they collectively figured out how to combine themselves into more complex organisms. The atheist argues some of those multi-cell organisms figured out how to specialize and perform specific functions within a greater organism. Some decided their function should be an eye within the more complex organism. Others decided their function should be an ear. Enough of them agreed what their specific functions should be to create the first animal. Eventually they figured out how to work together to form something as complex as a human being. I can't help but think that it takes a much larger leap of faith than to simply believe there is an intelligent being that designed everything we see. One who is greater than I. I personally am a strong believer in intelligent design theory. This is one reason why I believe in God (our creator).

You can choose whichever side of the spectrum you fall between being an atheist and believing in a Creator, but once you have made the decision between believing in a God (a Creator) or not (being an atheist), you need to decide what your stance is on religion. I personally think a creator would want to share His message to His creation, and I think the Bible is God's holy word and the mechanism God chose to deliver His message to His creation. I believe the universe was created by a single God (I do not believe in multiple gods). As a result, I chose a monotheistic religion. There are three major monotheistic religions in the world. I choose Christianity over the other two monotheistic religions because I believe Christianity uniquely includes the complete and true word of God. Christianity is the only religion (including both the Old and New Testaments taken together). This is essentially why I believe the way I do, but I would encourage you to do your own research. It's important you get comfortable with what you believe and (if you believe in a creator) which religion you chose to associate with. We all have our own free will to choose. God wants you to worship and honor Him as a choice, not as a command.

Many believe the Christian religion is the most exclusive religion on earth. They believe this because Christians say the only way to get into heaven is through salvation in Jesus. What strikes me is all three of the world's monotheistic religions are either looking for someone to save them, or the second coming of Jesus. The Jews are still looking for their messiah, and Islam recognizes Jesus as a great prophet. Islam is anticipating His second coming as the return of a great prophet. This is interesting because, by definition, a prophet cannot lie. Understanding this, we need to really understand what Jesus said about himself. What was His testimony, and who did he claim to be? Jesus said He was the Alpha and the Omega. He said He existed, along with God, before the world's creation, and He said He would be killed and be resurrected. In fact, His own testimony caused the Jews to crucify Him for the cardinal sin of blasphemy. There can be no doubt about who Jesus claimed himself to be. He claimed Himself to be none other than the son of God and the Jewish Messiah.

Islam doesn't recognize Jesus as the son of God, so they do not accept His own testimony. In essence, they are calling Jesus a liar. With respect to Islamic tradition, you can't recognize someone as being a prophet, but also consider them to be a liar. Jews, on the other hand, don't recognize Jesus as really anything at all. They don't really know what to think about Him. Jews assert Jesus never fulfilled any of their ancient prophecies. Christians believe Jesus fulfilled every one of the ancient prophecies concerning the Messiah in the Old Testament. With respect to the Jews, they are still looking for their Messiah to come riding into Jerusalem upon a donkey. Christianity believes Jesus already presented himself to the Jews 2,000 years ago. They rejected Him as their Messiah. They hung Him on the cross because He claimed to be the son of God. Christians are eagerly awaiting the second coming of Jesus.

The fact of the matter is you have been endowed with your own free will to make your own choice about how you believe and what you believe in. As I stated earlier, God doesn't want people to follow Him as a command. He wants people to follow Him as a choice. I have presented some reasons within this book as to why I believe the way I do, but I encourage you to do your own research and use your own free will to decide what you believe.

GOD'S CALLING

IT'S IMPORTANT TO UNDERSTAND GOD has charged Christians with a very important job. Jesus provided this great commission to h_s apostles.

> For you will be a witness for him to all men of what you have seen and heard." ~ **Acts 22:15**

In addition, Jesus empowered His followers to do exactly what he was asking them to do.

> "Most certainly I tell you, he who believes in me, the works that I do, he will do also; and he will do greater works than these, because I am going to my Father. Whatever you will ask in my name, I will do it, that the Father may be glorified in the Son. If you will ask anything in my name, I will do it." ~ **John 14:12-14**

This verse is amazing! What Jesus is telling us is through His mercy and grace He provided the ability to do the same acts that He was performing – including healings and miracles! Once we become Christians, we cannot ignore this great commission. There have been numerous debates about the ability to receive our salvation through our works and whether the works we perform are required for our salvation. The Bible makes it clear we do not receive salvation through our works. Our salvation is granted only through the blood of Jesus and the mercy of God. God makes it very clear salvation is provided through God's mercy and grace alone so that no man may boast in it.

> For by grace you have been saved through faith, and that not of yourselves; it is the gift of God, not of works, that no one would boast. For we are his workmanship, created in Christ Jesus for good works, which God prepared before that we would walk in them. ~ **Ephesians 2: 8-10**

This verse very clearly shows it is not the works we perform here on earth that allow us to earn our salvation. Salvation is not earned. It is a gift bestowed upon us through God's great mercy, and it is presented to those that earnestly believe Jesus is who he claimed to be (the son of God) and His sacrifice on the cross atoned for our sins. We can never lose our salvation.

> I give eternal life to them. They will never perish, and no one will snatch them out of my hand. My Father who has given them to me is greater than all. No one is able to snatch them out of my Father's hand. I and the Father are one." ~ **John 10:28-30**

Once we become saved our entire being changes. We will perform good works due to our salvation in Jesus (this is called sanctification). We can never earn or lose our salvation through works. The Bible makes it clear we have all fallen short of the glory of God. If we want more evidence, it is not through works that we are permitted to enter heaven, we need look no further than the example provided at Jesus' crucifixion of two criminals crucified on either side of Him. (Luke 23: 26-43)

There were two criminals crucified with Jesus. One of those criminals spent his time hurling insults at Jesus but the other criminal rebuked him and simply asked Jesus to remember him when He came into His kingdom. Neither of these criminals would have done anything in their lives to deserve to be saved, but Jesus' response to the criminal that asked Him to remember him when He came into His kingdom was simply this, "Truly I tell you, today you will be with me in paradise" (verse 43). We can conclude it is through the combination of the criminal's faith and God's mercy that the criminal received his salvation. Works have nothing to do with your salvation other than to say those saved will naturally perform good works because of their salvation. They will have a natural desire to want to perform good works once they realize the sacrifice made for them and the true nature of God's mercy provided to them. Each of the criminals crucified on either side of Jesus had different outcomes. The criminal that hurled insults at Jesus died in his sin. The criminal that asked Jesus to remember him when He came into His kingdom displayed his faith that Jesus was the son of God, and it was simply this faith that permitted him to be saved and enter God's presence in paradise.

> What good is it, my brothers, if a man says he has faith, but has no works? Can faith save him? And if a brother or sister is naked and in lack of daily food, and one of you tells them, "Go in peace. Be warmed and filled;" yet you didn't give them the things the body needs, what good is it? Even so faith, if it has

no works, is dead in itself. Yes, a man will say, "You have faith, and I have works." Show me your faith without works, and I will show you my faith by my works. You believe that God is one. You do well. The demons also believe, and shudder. But do you want to know, vain man, that faith apart from works is dead? ~ **James 2:14-20**

This passage from the letter of James indicates works we perform are important and are not ignored by God. The verse doesn't say works are required for salvation but does point out true Christians display their faith through performing good works. The Bible makes it clear Christians will perform good works and bear good fruit. The Bible also provides some clear warnings to those who fail to acknowledge Jesus.

Everyone therefore who confesses me before men, I will also confess him before my Father who is in heaven. But whoever denies me before men, I will also deny him before my Father who is in heaven." ~ **Matthew 10:32-33**

For whoever will be ashamed of me and of my words, of him will the Son of Man be ashamed, when he comes in his glory, and the glory of the Father, and of the holy angels. ~ **Luke 9:26**

If we profess to be Christian, we must openly confess knowing Jesus and believing in His message. If we fail to do this, we have been warned about how we will be dealt with on the day of judgment.

My life has been blessed. I have witnessed many miraculous answers to prayer. I have fostered a close relationship with God through countless hours of prayer and spending time reading God's word. Many of the miraculous events that I have had the opportunity to witness have come during my most active times in church. As a result, I think it's very important Christians remain active in church and take on active roles within the church. I believe an active church life presents many opportunities for Christians to see how God works. If we fail to have an active church life, we have fewer opportunities for fellowship with other Christians. In addition, we have fewer opportunities available for God to work within our lives and reveal His glory to us.

THE WATCHMAN

WE HAVE THE RESPONSIBILITY TO be a watchman for other believers. God tasks us with the responsibility to look out for others. If we see something leading to their harm, we are to act. God communicated this to Ezekiel in Ezekiel chapter 33.

> Yahweh's word came to me, saying, "Son of man, speak to the children of your people, and tell them, 'When I bring the sword on a land, and the people of the land take a man from among them, and set him for their watchman; if, when he sees the sword come on the land, he blows the trumpet, and warns the people; then whoever hears the sound of the trumpet, and doesn't heed the warning, if the sword comes, and takes him away, his blood will be on his own head. He heard the sound of the trumpet, and didn't take warning. His blood will be on him; whereas if he had heeded the warning, he would have delivered his soul. But if the watchman sees the sword come, and doesn't blow the trumpet, and the people aren't warned, and the sword comes, and takes any person from among them; he is taken away in his iniquity, but his blood I will require at the watchman's hand." So you, son of man: I have set you a watchman to the house of Israel. Therefore, hear the word from my mouth, and give them warnings from me. When I tell the wicked, 'O wicked man, you will surely die,' and you don't speak to warn the wicked from his way; that wicked man will die in his iniquity, but I will require his blood at your hand. Nevertheless, if you warn the wicked of his way to turn from it, and he doesn't turn from his way; he will die in his iniquity, but you have delivered your soul.'" **Ezekiel 33:1-9**

Ezekiel tells us we have a responsibility to act. If we see something causing someone's harm our duty is to make them aware. If you are a Christian, you are a watchman. Our collective responsibility is to spread His gospel (good news) to the ends of the earth. We are currently living in a wicked generation. Our duty is to actively spread the good news of His gospel to the entire world. Ezekiel's message continues:

As for you, son of man, the children of your people talk about you by the walls and in the doors of the houses, and speak to one another, everyone to his brother, saying, 'Please come and hear what the word is that comes out from Yahweh.' They come to you as the people come, and they sit before you as my people, and they hear your words, but don't do them; for with their mouth they show much love, but their heart goes after their gain. Behold, you are to them as a very lovely song of one who has a pleasant voice and can play well on an instrument; for they hear your words, but they don't do them. "When this comes to pass—behold, it comes—then they will know that a prophet has been among them." ~ **Ezekiel 33:30-33**

The above Bible verse makes it clear the people Ezekiel was delivering his message to were not receptive to him. Sure, they heard the words, but their hearts were not receptive enough to repent. Ezekiel was still provided the command to send the message to this group of people even though God told Ezekiel his message would have no impact on them. Likewise, we are commanded to deliver the message of the gospel to all people. Only God can work within the hearts of people we witness to make them receptive to the message. Our responsibility is simply to speak the message to all people and leave it to God to open their hearts to be receptive to the message we share with them. As Christians we collectively have a responsibility to carry God's message to the ends of the earth so all may be provided an opportunity to be saved. We know God is love, and we know that God is perfectly just. We are to be God's hands and feet in this broken and wicked world. God wants us to look at the many examples contained within the Bible displaying how He dealt with Israel in the Old Testament and how Jesus dealt with humanity in the New Testament. These examples point to a God whose very nature is love, and who embodies perfect justice. God's desire for us is to reflect His nature as we fulfill our responsibility of being a watchman. When we rebuke a brother or sister in Christ, we need to be careful to do so in love and without judgment. We must also understand we do not share the same perspective God has when it comes to His perfect justice. We must have confidence in God's ability to bring justice to a broken and imperfect world and we must not be judgmental toward other people using what limited perspective we might have.

ISRAEL

ISRAEL IS GOD'S CHOSEN NATION and God has maintained a very active role in Israel's progression as a nation. When they followed His decrees and gave Him their unadulterated worship God caused Israel to flourish, but God punished Israel when they failed to follow His decrees and give him their unadulterated worship. During the reign of King David, and early in the reign of King Solomon, Israel flourished as a nation, they expanded their territory and built God's temple. They flourished because they were wholeheartedly following God's decrees and providing Him their unadulterated worship. Later in King Solomon's reign Israel started to follow other gods. As a result, God decided to punish Israel by splitting the nation into two kingdoms (the northern kingdom of Israel and the southern kingdom of Judah). Of the twelve original tribes of Israel God caused ten tribes to rebel against Solomon's son, King Rehoboam. Those ten tribes of Israel split apart from the other two tribes of Israel, and they formed the northern kingdom of Israel. The remaining two tribes remained loyal to King Rehoboam, and they formed the southern kingdom of Judah.

Throughout Israel's history God followed a pattern consistent with mercy and love. Ultimately, however, it became necessary to destroy the northern kingdom of Israel as well as the southern kingdom of Judah. The way God dealt with the nation of Israel is documented within the Old Testament of the Bible. He gave them every opportunity to repent and return to Him before finally destroying them. Time and time again God sent Israel judges, prophets, and warnings. He provided them defeats in battle when they chose to rely upon their own strength (or the strength of other nations around them) rather than trusting in Him for their protection. He sent them warnings about what would happen if they continued to intermarry with the other nations around them, thereby mixing their purity with the other nations, defiling themselves. He warned them about what would happen if they continued to worship other false gods and idols rather than providing Him their unadulterated worship (a position only He deserves in our lives).

God's determination to destroy both the northern and southern kingdoms of Israel centered around their unwillingness to give Him the central place in their lives. Neither kingdom worshiped God in the way

He commanded. God told Israel through His commandments they must not follow other Gods, but both nations were following other Gods at the time of their destruction. When God finally determined to destroy them, His actions were as justifiable and merciful as possible. First, He sent them warnings through the prophets; then He allowed them to endure small losses of territory, then He allowed them to suffer harsher defeats in battle. When they still didn't get the message to repent and return to Him, He caused division amongst them. He split the nation in two (into the northern kingdom of Israel and the southern kingdom of Judah). He destroyed the northern kingdom first. He permitted the Assyrians to destroy the northern kingdom of Israel. The ten northern tribes of Israel remain disbursed throughout the world today because of the Assyrian devastation.

Even after the destruction of the northern kingdom, the southern kingdom failed to repent and return to Him. As a result, He found it necessary to also destroy the southern kingdom of Judah. Even in destruction, He left a remnant of Israel's population. He allowed them to go into captivity within Babylon for a finite period (seventy years). He didn't disperse them in the same way He dispersed the ten northern tribes of Israel. Furthermore, when they were in captivity in Babylon Judah still served as a witness to the Babylonians. Have you ever read the book of Daniel? It's one of my favorite books of the Bible. It shows God used the people of Judah during the time of their captivity. It shows He still had a great purpose for His people even during their captivity. When Daniel began asking questions about when they would become a nation again, God answered him in a miraculous manner (foretelling the very number of years Israel would remain a nation and foretelling the very year that Jesus would be crucified for the atonement of all sin). He returned the remnant back to Judah after seventy years of captivity in Babylon. The point I'm trying to make is absolutely everything your Heavenly Father does is done as an act of mercy and love. God showed His love to Israel but also displayed His discipline toward Israel because Israel failed to repent and return to Him. King David knew of God's great mercy. King David displayed this after his sin of taking a census of Israel (a sin of national pride) as he chose to accept correction and rebuke at the hands of God rather than at the hands of man.

> When David rose up in the morning, Yahweh's word came to the prophet Gad, David's seer, saying, "Go and speak to David, 'Yahweh says, "I offer you three things. Choose one of them, that I may do it to you."'" So God came to David, and told him, and said to him, "Shall seven years of famine come to you in your land? Or will you flee three months before your foes while they pursue you? Or shall there be three days' pestilence in your land? Now answer, and consider what answer I shall return to him who sent me." David said to Gad, "I am in distress. **Let us fall now into Yahweh's hand; for his mercies are great. Let me not fall into man's hand.**" *[emphasis added]* - **2 Samuel 24: 11-14**

David selected a judgment delivered at the hands of the Lord because he knew God would be more merciful than man would be. He knew this because God is love! Everything God does includes some level of mercy and love. God makes a distinction between His people and those that don't believe in Him. You can be assured this is true. God follows a similar pattern of how He dealt with Israel in the Old Testament and how he deals with His believers in the current age. This provides testimony to God's unchanging nature. God's laws don't change. What He declares wrong will always be wrong. What He declares Right will always be Right.

We must also understand God didn't desire to bring destruction upon Israel. We can be assured of this by what we find in the Bible. God split the nation of Israel into the northern and southern kingdoms due to King Solomon's disobedience. Solomon's many wives eventually lead his heart away from God. Over time Solomon's wives persuaded him to bring idolatry to Israel. When God made the decision to split Israel into two nations, He intended to do two things.

- Humble and correct Judah (the southern kingdom) as it remained loyal to Solomon's son (King Rehoboam).
- Give the ten northern tribes of Israel over to Jeroboam as their king so he could rule those tribes in a manner consistent with God's commands.

When God gave the ten northern tribes to Jeroboam, He made a conditional promise to him.

> "It shall be, if you will listen to all that I command you, and will walk in my ways, and do that which is right in my eyes, to keep my statutes and my commandments, as David my servant did; that I will be with you, and will build you a sure house, as I built for David, and will give Israel to you." ~1 **King 11:38**

This verse contains the conditional promise made to king Jeroboam. We can see from that conditional promise God originally intended to continue to richly bless Israel with His love rather than destroy Israel. He split the kingdom of Israel so He could be merciful to the ten northern tribes of Israel while correcting the southern kingdom of Judah. He split Israel as a nation and caused two tribes to remain loyal to King Rehoboam to keep His promise to David by making him and his descendants an enduring dynasty over Israel, but God intended to humble and correct the Southern kingdom while he would allow the northern kingdom to flourish under king Jeroboam's reign (under God's conditional promise).

King Jeroboam immediately decided to take the ten northern tribes into idolatry. As a result, Jeroboam never met the conditions of God's promise made to him. Within Jeroboam's reign he almost immediately created two golden calf idols and set them up in two northern cities (the cities of Bethel and Dan). He did this because he felt fear and doubt. His fear centered around potential rebellion against him. He felt people from the northern tribes of Israel would rebel against him if they were required to travel back to the southern kingdom of Judah to worship their God at His holy temple. Jeroboam's doubt came from a lack of faith in God's promise to him. Ultimately the combination of fear and doubt caused him to take the northern ten tribes down the path of idolatry to their ultimate destruction. From these Bible verses, however, we can see God intended to be merciful and loving toward Israel. The sinful nature of man sent both the northern and southern kingdoms of Israel down the path to their ultimate destruction. (Chapters 11 and 12 of 1 Kings provide details.)

What we can learn from the above Bible verses is God made conditional promises that were not met by king Jeroboam (see verse 11:38). It was not God's desire to destroy either the nation of Israel or Judah. His desire was to correct and humble the southern kingdom while He continued to richly bless the ten northern tribes under King Jeroboam's reign. Even in destroying both the northern and southern kingdom He allowed a remnant to remain.

God always keeps His promises. You can see this in the way He dealt with the nation of Israel. Israel was chosen by God to show the world His nature. We can look at the examples He provided us in how he dealt with Israel to see how He will deal with us. When we choose to start to walk away from Him, He will lovingly try to draw us back to Him. If we continue to walk in the opposite direction from God, we can expect God will do everything to try to get our attention to repent and return to Him. God is in absolute love with those who choose to accept Him as their savior. You can expect He will rebuke you should you choose to walk in a direction counter to his purpose for your life.

THE FIRE ON BLANCHE AVENUE

I WANT TO SHARE WITH you a story my mother shared with me as I was growing up. This story provides clear evidence God performs miracles on behalf of His followers through their prayers. I will share this story with you in the next two chapters of this book told from my mother's point of view as she has conveyed the story to me during my childhood and my young Christian Walk.

After my father's death my mother needed help keeping up with the rental properties she and my father owned. Since Mark and I were the only ones who didn't own a home, we packed our things and went to live with my mother at her house on Blanche Avenue in Cincinnati. We contacted our insurance representative when we decided to move into the house to figure out what we needed to do about our fire insurance policies. He informed us we would need to cancel our insurance policy, because the house was in my mother's name and would be covered under her insurance policy. He said insurance companies would not pay for two policies for a single house in the event of a fire. Consequently, Mark and I cancelled our policy.

Mark and I lived with my mother for quite some time, but eventually we decided we needed to obtain a place of our own. Mother was steadily recovering from the death of my father, and we decided it was time for us to move on with our lives. Mark and I decided the best course of action was to move into an apartment close to mother so we could continue to help her with the rental property and provide a comfortable measure of distance for our families. After a bit of searching, we found a beautiful town house close to mom's house. Although old, the house was well maintained and had spacious rooms with high ceilings. It suited our needs perfectly and Mark was ready to move in right away. Even though the house would be available on December 17th, I convinced Mark to wait. I wanted to wait until after Christmas to move into the new house. I really wanted to spend the holiday season with my mother, in her house, one last time.

In retrospect, the decision to delay our move turned out to be a bad one. My mother's house caught fire on the night of December 17th. The exact date the new town house would have been available to move into.

Had we decided to move into the town house that day all our belongings would have been moved out of my mother's house before the fire. This wasn't the case, however, and all our material possessions were in the house when it caught fire. The fire was so severe that five fire trucks were dispatched to battle it. It even made the local news – both television and newspaper. Nearly all our possessions were destroyed. Our only other major possession (our car) had been wrecked just weeks prior to the fire while parked on my aunt's street.

Mark and I had to start our lives all over again. You know, I never really thought about how expensive it would be to replace all the items lost in a fire. When you stop and think about all the items in your homes, the clothes, the toys, the furniture, and everything else, it really adds up to an astronomical sum of money. We had accumulated all these possessions over the years, writing small checks for each item. When you accumulate items a little at a time you really lose sight of the total value of those items until you are faced with replacing them all at once. It was going to prove very difficult for us to start over from scratch. In addition, the reporters who documented the fire in the local newspaper and local television news programs got all the details wrong. They had inaccurate address and phone number information for Mark and me, so if anyone wanted to send donations to help us through these difficult times, they would have a very difficult time trying to track us down. I always felt it was a bit odd that all our information was reported inaccurately. I oftentimes wonder if the Holy Spirit wasn't involved in this as well. What better way to show Mark and I He would provide for all our needs than to isolate us from help from the news media and external means of support?

Through all of this, Mark and I never felt an ounce of worry or discomfort. Mark and I were both young and Mark had a great job at General Motors. In addition, we had turned the matter over to God through prayer. We were sure that God would provide for our family. I can remember one instance specifically about the inner peace that I had throughout the entire ordeal. One morning after the fire, I was walking down to a laundry facility in one of mother's apartment buildings. I was humming a church hymn, "He's able, He's able, I know my Lord is able…" I was collecting the coins from the washing machines and thinking about the fire and how much we had lost. It occurred to me that Mark and I were really in a mess. Everything was going to be so expensive to replace. Mom was underinsured and we had cancelled our homeowner's policy. As a result, we didn't receive that much help from the insurance company. I wasn't really worrying about how we would replace it all, but I was thinking we were in a messy situation. A small voice told me not to worry, everything was under control.

God did, in fact, have everything under control. God provided all our needs after the fire. The outpouring of love from everyone was truly remarkable. For instance, the day Mark returned to work his boss met him at the door to tell him to go home and provide for his family. He told Mark he had no business being at work when his family had no place to live, and he didn't want to see him back at the assembly plant until after the holidays were over and his family was settled. He assured Mark he didn't have to worry about anything other than his family. His job would be taken care of. People from the assembly plant made sure Mark and I attended the Christmas party where they presented us with a gift of about $2,500. Donations poured in from people who worked with Mark. It was a unified effort by workers who empathized with our situation and wanted to do whatever they could to help us get back on our feet as quickly as possible. We were truly thankful for everything we received and were deeply touched by the outpouring of love from everyone. We received numerous donations of gifts, clothes, and other items from people we never knew. One of the amazing things was most of the sizes and colors were perfect. Some clothing was old, but most of everything we received fit perfectly. The color and design were perfect. It was obvious to me God was directing this entire effort and was prompting people to provide all the items we needed. I don't want to make it sound like absolutely everything was perfect. Some items we received were incorrect and a lot of stuff was old and sometimes not useful to our family, but there were unmistakable signs God's hand was at work. This was a miracle coordinated by God. We received everything we needed through the numerous donations. God provided all our needs through the generous outpouring of gifts and donations.

It truly was amazing. I remember one incident specifically. One morning I walked over to the house of the fire chief of Cincinnati. The fire chief lived only a few doors down from us. As I said earlier, the newspapers and television news reports didn't have any of our information correct, so most people didn't know where to send donations. As I was talking to the fire chief, a gentleman came to the house. He said he was a doctor, and he had a donation for our family. The trunk of his car was filled with wrapped Christmas presents for our family. It bothered him that our children had lost all their toys and clothes in the fire, and he felt led to provide us with gifts for Christmas. As we talked, I asked for his name. He said I didn't need to know his name, only that this was something he wanted to do for us. I am truly grateful to that gentleman for his outpouring of love during a difficult time in our lives. I believe he was led by the Holy Spirit because every gift we received from him was perfect. All the items of clothing fit each of us perfectly. There wasn't a single item that didn't fit or wasn't the right color. These were indeed gifts from God!

There was another incident that stuck out in my mind. After Mark and I moved into the town house, we continued to receive gifts and packages that were providing for our needs. I was truly grateful, but one night I was in the town house, and I noticed one wall had a fireplace running down the center of the wall. There were two tall narrow windows on either side of the fireplace. They weren't standard sized windows. I remember thinking as I prayed; "I wonder what I can do about those windows. We have so much other stuff to replace. I can't possibly afford to go out and buy custom drapes for those windows. What am I going to do about that?" I didn't share that thought with anyone. One morning I went to our Bible study class. As I was walking into the class one of my friends stopped me. She was carrying a package, a delivery from her mother to me. She said her mother had been praying one night, and she received a clear message from God that I could use these drapes. She said she was told, through prayer, she should go up to her attic and find these drapes. Her mother found these drapes and dry-cleaned them for me. Not only were they beautiful, but they were perfect for the two windows! I didn't even need to hem them! The colors were perfect for the room, taupe mixed with soft green and orange hues. To be honest, I don't think I could have gone out and purchased a nicer pair of drapes for that room. It was amazing how God supplied all our needs after the fire on Blanche Avenue. He truly does take care of his followers. Philippians 4:19 (KJV) says, "But my God shall supply all your needs according to his riches in glory by Christ Jesus."

God truly did respond to all our needs during this difficult time in our lives. He did it through the tremendous outpouring of love from other people. He made sure every need was met. This was a difficult situation for us. Mark and I have always been extremely proud people. Mark especially hates to take gifts from others, and he felt very uncomfortable about receiving all the gifts and donations from everyone who showed genuine concern regarding our situation. Everyone was so generous. The outpouring of gifts and love was truly remarkable. Mark had a difficult time because he never felt we were destitute throughout this incident. He was young and had a good job. We had lost nearly everything, but there was plenty of time to recover from such a devastating fire. Looking back on this incident, I really think the Lord used this as a learning experience for both of us. I think He really wanted to show us he could provide for all our needs. Up to this point in our lives Mark and I always felt self-sufficient. Through this incident we learned we could rely upon the lord for everything we needed. We learned the lord is a wonderful provider for our needs and we could rely upon Him for everything.

A ROOM UNTOUCHED BY FIRE

MARK'S MOTHER DIDN'T HAVE ANY income at the time of the fire on Blanche Avenue. She didn't have any place to live and had been living with Mark, Peggy, and Skip (her children) for quite some time. I knew this wasn't the best situation for her and I began to pray about it. I asked Jesus to help find a permanent home for her. I also asked the Lord to help provide a means of income for her since she didn't have any money of her own. A few days after I prayed, the Lord gave me an answer to my prayer. I was talking with my next-door neighbor about the situation, and she told me she knew of a new program through the Metropolitan Housing Authority for low-income housing. She thought Mark's mother would probably qualify for the low-income apartment. She suggested I investigate this option. In addition, she thought I should also contact Social Security for assistance. I knew this was an answer to my prayers, so I began to investigate these options. I called the Metropolitan Housing Authority and the Department of Social Security and asked them what would be required for a person to qualify for their programs. I was told I needed the death certificate of Stella's first husband and needed to be able to prove Stella had no other means of income or support from anyone else. I could prove Stella had no income, but I knew Stella was still married to Mark's stepfather. Mark's stepfather left Stella sometime after their marriage, but they hadn't legally divorced.

I knew I had to find out where Mark's stepfather was so that I could prove he was no longer providing a means of support to Stella. I had no idea where to begin the search and neither did Mark nor anybody else. I prayed to Jesus that we might be led to find the whereabouts of Mark's stepfather. My prayer was answered. It was amazing how God opened doors for us and guided our search to find Mark's stepfather quickly. I can't remember exactly how we tracked him down, but I know the search was much easier than I anticipated it would be. We found he had been living with his daughter in Kentucky. Furthermore, Stella informed us they had established a will together shortly after they were married, and this will had never been modified. I contacted the daughter in Kentucky only to find she was very evasive. She didn't want to answer any of my questions regarding her father.

She did, however, indicate her father had lived with her and he had passed away some time ago. I informed her all I wanted from her was a copy of her father's death certificate so I could prove Stella had no means of supporting herself and was not being supported by anyone else. The daughter refused to give me the requested copy of the death certificate. I had a feeling she was concerned I was going to sue for whatever was left from her father's estate after he passed away. She knew I had a copy of the will and was afraid my call was a prelude to a court battle.

I informed the daughter many times I wanted the copy of the death certificate only to prove Stella had no means of support, and I had no interest in her father's estate, but she continued to be evasive and wouldn't provide a copy of her father's death certificate. I hung up the phone with no resolution. It seemed I had run into a brick wall. I didn't let it discourage me, though, because I had been working in an attorney's office prior to the birth of the twins. I remained close with the attorneys, so I contacted one of them and asked what I should do about this situation. We had a letter written from his law firm requesting the death certificate. I tried the tactic, but the daughter still refused to provide a copy of her father's death certificate. Again, I contacted my attorney and asked him what I should do. He indicated he would help me out. He wrote a letter informing the daughter that she was to appear in court. He informed the daughter her refusal to provide her father's death certificate left us no option but to sue for the proceeds of her father's estate. He informed the daughter we had a copy of Stella's will, and she was required to provide a copy of her father's death certificate. He informed her failure to provide her father's death certificate would be a criminal offense and she could be held liable for contempt of court.

A court hearing was set, and I collected all the required papers that would allow us to litigate this court case on behalf of Stella. I placed all these important documents in a drawer within a chest in our dining room. It seemed we had everything we needed to litigate the case and would be able to eventually provide some income for Mark's mother. About a week prior to the court date the house caught on fire. The fire broke out at night, so we were all upstairs asleep. My mother and I woke up and realized the house was engulfed in flames. I ran into the twins' room to get Tom out of bed. Mom had already taken Tami downstairs. There was very heavy smoke in the house. The smoke upstairs was so thick I placed a blanket over Tom's head, so he wouldn't breathe the smoke into his lungs. I ran downstairs, crossed the living room floor and went out the front door of the house.

*These are the stairs I walked down as I was exiting
the house carrying Tom in my arms."*

Someone else must have called the fire department because trucks were already pulling up to the house as I was leaving. I thanked God the firefighters had arrived so quickly. I had no time to waste though. I knew we had important papers in the dining room. We needed those papers to litigate Stella's court case. The fire looked bad, so I rushed over to my neighbor's house and called our church prayer chain from there. I informed the prayer chain our house was on fire and the fire looked bad. I asked them to pray for one thing. I didn't really care about the rest of the house, but I asked them to make sure to pray the dining room didn't burn. I told them I had important papers in the dining room, and they must not burn!

The fire was severe. I was told by some of the firemen, after the blaze had been extinguished, the fire was so intense one of their trucks sustained severe heat damage because it was parked too close to the house. Another fireman told me he was amazed I was able to exit the house in the way I had. He said when his firemen tried to enter the house through the same door I exited, only moments before, they could not enter that door of the house. He indicated the living room floor collapsed, and it was his opinion I walked across a carpet that had no floor under it. He said it was a miracle, both of us were alive. There was also evidence in the aftermath of the fire that showed how intense it must have been. My mother had a diamond-banded watch in a metal jewelry case. The metal jewelry box melted and the diamonds from the watch band were found encrusted in the melted metal case. This had been an extremely hot fire!

This is a photo taken after the fire had been extinguished, of the room adjacent to the dining room. This photo shows the floor I walked across when I exited the house that evening. You can see the floor fell through to the basement.

The amazing thing was the dining room of the house remained relatively untouched by the fire. It was close to Christmas, and the tree in our dining room was still green! In addition, the wax on the candles of the dining room table hadn't melted! How was it the fire was so hot that it melted a metal jewelry case and damaged a fire truck parked outside the house, but didn't melt the wax in the candles on the dining room table? When you really think about it there is but one explanation; this was a miracle. God protected that room throughout the fire so it wouldn't burn. The adjacent rooms on either side of the dining room were destroyed by fire, but the dining room itself was virtually untouched by the flames. We also found the legal papers we had been praying for without a mark on them. They didn't have any water or smoke damage! The documents were perfectly legible. It was as if God placed His hand over that room in our house and said, "This room will not burn."

This photo shows the dining room, and the chest containing the legal documents I was praying for.

With the legal papers in hand, we were able to litigate Stella's court case and were able to obtain a place for her to live and a means of support for her. It is amazing that, as intense as this fire was, one room was spared. It just so happened the room sparred was the exact same room we were praying for. If you are having a hard time convincing yourself this was coincidental, there is a very good reason for that: nothing about this fire was coincidental. Nothing happened by chance. All the other rooms were destroyed except the dining room. Rooms adjacent to the dining room were destroyed by the flames. I talked to the firemen, and they had never seen anything like this fire. They said it was one of the most intense fires they had ever encountered (certainly for a residential home anyway). The house should have been completely destroyed. They had no explanation for why the dining room was untouched by the fire. This was yet another example of God's quick answer to prayer in my life.

More than 20 years later Mark and I took a vacation. Mark and I began talking with a gentleman sitting next to us at one of the locations we were visiting. I found out he had been a fire chief in one of the suburbs of Cincinnati. I began telling him this story about the miraculous fire on Blanche Avenue. He said he had heard about that fire. He said the fire was somewhat legendary at the firehouse where he worked. He asked me if I knew about the lady who carried the baby over a carpet that had no floor underneath it. I told him I was that lady and showed him a picture of my son. We had a very interesting conversation about the fire and the way Jesus has worked in my life.

Photo of our house on Blanche Avenue taken after the fire.

This photo was taken of the bedroom from the apartment that was attached to our house.

These photos shows the kitchen of the apartment that was attached to our house on Blanche Avenue.

This picture was taken of our kitchen after the fire.

These pictures were taken of one of the upstairs bedrooms in the house on Blanche Avenue after the fire.

THE RISE AND FALL OF NATIONS

WE CAN BE ASSURED GOD pays attention to the affairs of how governments and influential leaders conduct themselves. He pays attention to how they use the authority He alone permits them to have. We are living His story. You have a role to play in His story. Even in predicting the rise and fall of nations, the Bible makes clear how we, as individuals, can be called to play a role in the purposes of God. Chapter two in the book of Daniel provides evidence of God's sovereignty over the nations of the earth. And notice, too, the role Daniel plays in hearing and speaking God's word. This story is so important it is worth reading all of Daniel chapter two:

DANIEL CHAPTER 2

In the second year of the reign of Nebuchadnezzar, Nebuchadnezzar dreamed dreams; and his spirit was troubled, and his sleep went from him. Then the king commanded that the magicians, the enchanters, the sorcerers, and the Chaldeans be called to tell the king his dreams. So they came in and stood before the king. The king said to them, "I have dreamed a dream, and my spirit is troubled to know the dream." Then the Chaldeans spoke to the king in the Syrian language, "O king, live forever! Tell your servants the dream, and we will show the interpretation." The king answered the Chaldeans, "The thing has gone from me. If you don't make known to me the dream and its interpretation, you will be cut in pieces, and your houses will be made a dunghill. But if you show the dream and its interpretation, you will receive from me gifts, rewards, and great honor. Therefore, show me the dream and its interpretation." They answered the second time and said, "Let the king tell his servants the dream, and we will show the interpretation." The king answered, "I know of a certainty that you are trying to gain time, because you see the thing has gone from me. But if you don't make known to me the dream, there is but one law for you; for you have prepared lying and corrupt words to speak before me, until the situation changes. Therefore, tell me the dream, and I will know that you can show me its interpretation." The Chaldeans answered before the king, and said, "There is not a man on the earth who can show the king's matter, because no king, lord, or ruler, has asked such a thing of any magician, enchanter, or Chaldean. It is a rare thing that the king requires, and there is no other who can show it before the king, except the gods, whose dwelling is not with flesh." Because of this, the king was angry and very furious, and commanded that all the wise men of Babylon be destroyed. So the decree went out, and the wise men were to be slain. They sought Daniel and his companions to be slain. Then Daniel returned answer with counsel and prudence to Arioch the captain of the king's guard, who had gone out to kill the wise men of Babylon. He answered Arioch the king's captain, "Why is the decree so urgent from the king?" Then Arioch made the thing known to Daniel. 16 Daniel went in, and desired of the king that he would appoint him a time, and he would show the king the interpretation. Then Daniel went to his house and made the thing known to Hananiah, Mishael, and Azariah, his companions: that they would desire mercies of the God of heaven concerning this secret; that Daniel and his companions would not perish with the rest of the wise men of Babylon. Then the secret was revealed to Daniel in a vision of the night. Then Daniel blessed the God of heaven. Daniel answered, "Blessed be the name of God forever and ever; for wisdom and might are his. He changes the times and the seasons. He removes kings and sets up kings. He gives wisdom to the wise, and knowledge to those who have understanding. He reveals the deep and secret things. He knows what is in the darkness, and the light dwells with him. I thank you and praise you, O God of my fathers, who have given me wisdom and might, and have now made known to me what we desired of you; for you have made known to us the king's matter."

DANIEL INTERPRETS THE DREAM

Therefore, Daniel went in to Arioch, whom the king had appointed to destroy the wise men of Babylon. He went and said this to him: "Don't destroy the wise men of Babylon. Bring me in before the king, and I will show to the king the interpretation." Then Arioch brought in Daniel before the king in haste and said this to him: "I have found a man of the children of the captivity of Judah who will make known to the king the interpretation." The king answered Daniel, whose name was Belteshazzar, "Are you able to make known to me the dream which I have seen, and its interpretation?" Daniel answered before the king, and said, "The secret which the king has demanded can't be shown to the king by wise men, enchanters, magicians, or soothsayers; but there is a God in heaven who reveals secrets, and he has made known to king Nebuchadnezzar what will be in the latter days. Your dream, and the visions of your head on your bed, are these: "As for you, O king, your thoughts came on your bed, what should happen hereafter; and he who reveals secrets has made known to you what will happen. But as for me, this secret is not revealed to me for any wisdom that I have more than any living, but with the intent that the interpretation may be made known to the king, and that you may know the thoughts of your heart. "You, O king, saw, and behold, a great image. This image, which was mighty, and whose brightness was excellent, stood before you; and its appearance was terrifying. As for this image, its head was fine gold, its breast and its arms of silver, its belly and its thighs of bronze, its legs of iron, its feet part of iron, and part of clay. You saw until a stone was cut out without hands, which struck the image on its feet that were of iron and clay and broke them in pieces. Then the iron, the clay, the bronze, the silver, and the gold were broken in pieces together, and became like the chaff of the summer threshing floors. The wind carried them away, so that no place was found for them. The stone that struck the image became a great mountain and filled the whole earth. "This is the dream; and we will tell its interpretation before the king. You, O king, are king of kings, to whom the God of heaven has given the kingdom, the power, the strength, and the glory. Wherever the children of men dwell, he has given the animals of the field and the birds of the sky into your hand and has made you rule over them all. You are the head of gold. "After you, another kingdom will arise that is inferior to you; and another third kingdom of bronze, which will rule over all the earth. The fourth kingdom will be strong as iron, because iron breaks into pieces and subdues all things; and as iron that crushes all these, it will break in pieces and crush. Whereas you saw the feet and toes, part of potters' clay, and part of iron, it will be a divided kingdom; but there will be in it the strength of the iron, because you saw the iron mixed with miry clay. As the toes of the feet were part of iron, and part of clay, so the kingdom will be partly strong, and partly broken. Whereas you saw the iron mixed with miry clay, they will mingle themselves with the seed of men; but they won't cling to one another, even as iron does not mix with clay. "In the days of those kings the God of heaven will set up a kingdom which will never be destroyed, nor will its sovereignty be left to another people; but it will break in pieces and consume all these kingdoms, and it will stand forever. Because you saw that a stone was cut out of the mountain without hands, and that it broke in pieces the iron, the bronze, the clay, the silver, and the gold; the great God has made known to the king what will happen hereafter. The dream is certain, and its interpretation sure." Then king Nebuchadnezzar fell on his face, worshiped Daniel, and commanded that they should offer an offering and sweet odors to him. The king answered to Daniel, and said, "Of a truth your God is the God of gods, and the Lord of kings, and a revealer of secrets, since you have been able to reveal this secret." Then the king made Daniel great, and gave him many great gifts, and made him rule over the whole province of Babylon, and to be chief governor over all the wise men of Babylon. Daniel requested the king, and he appointed Shadrach, Meshach, and Abednego over the affairs of the province of Babylon; but Daniel was in the king's gate.

The above set of prophetic Bible verses were written down at the time of the Babylonian empire (when King Nebuchadnezzar reigned). Daniel's interpretation of the dream predicted, in astonishing detail, the rise and fall of the following nations and kingdoms:

- The Babylonian empire
- The Medes and Persian empires
- Greece

- The Roman Empire
- A kingdom yet to rise (this will be the kingdom the antichrist reigns over)
- The kingdom that Jesus will reign over for eternity (ushered in by the stone striking the feet of the statue)[1]

From these prophetic Bible verses, we can see God's authority over the rise and fall of nations. We can see that these nations were pre-determined by God to rise to power and fall in a pre-determined pattern. As a result, we can have confidence that God is sovereign over all the nations of earth. He permits them to exist, and He alone sets the timing for their rise and fall.

Another book in the Old Testament provides an example of the mercy God displays toward even pagan nations. There is evidence within the Bible regarding how God seeks to correct pagan nations. We can see this illustrated within the first three chapters of the book of Jonah.

God asked Jonah to witness to Assyria to warn them of their impending doom. The nation of Assyria was considered an enemy of Israel, so Jonah didn't want to deliver God's warning to them. In fact, to avoid delivering the message of repentance to Assyria he immediately ran in the opposite direction. He tried with all his might to get as far away from Assyria as possible to avoid the direction God wanted him to go. God ultimately sent a great fish to swallow him. The fish spat him out on the shores of Assyria so that His message could be delivered. It never benefits us to run away from God. God's purpose will be fulfilled. It never benefits us to walk away from something God has placed on our hearts to accomplish on His behalf.

The Bible tells us upon hearing the warning Jonah sent them the Assyrians repented. As a result, God delayed his judgment against Assyria. The Assyrians wore sackcloth. They repented of their evil ways, and God spared that generation of Assyrians from His judgment and wrath. God permitted the destruction of Assyria at a later point in their history. The Bible tells us the Assyrians were used as God's tool to destroy the northern tribes of Israel, but it also tells us even though God used them as His tool of destruction to rebuke Israel He didn't condone all the actions taken by the Assyrians against Israel. They were brutal to the Israelites in their destruction. As a result, God later poured out his wrath on Assyria

---

[1]   "What is the meaning of Nebuchadnezzar's dream in Daniel 2?", Got Questions Ministries, *https://www.gotquestions.org/Nebuchadnezzars-dream.html*

for the atrocities done to Israel.

> Therefore, the Lord, Yahweh of Armies, says "My people who dwell in Zion, don't be afraid of the Assyrian, though he strike you with the rod, and lift up his staff against you, as Egypt did. For yet a very little while, and the indignation against you will be accomplished, and my anger will be directed to his destruction."
> **~ Isaiah 10: 24–25**

As pointed out in the book of Jonah, God relented from bringing his judgment on the generation of Assyrians that heard Jonah's message and heeded Jonah's warning to them. God displayed in the story of Jonah and Assyria He offers an opportunity to repent and return to him even for pagan nations. It wasn't God's desire to destroy Assyria at that time and He sent Jonah as a witness to proclaim a message of repentance. The Bible paints a picture of what happened to Assyria for us to see how He not only deals with the chosen nation of Israel but also pagan nations. He is merciful to both the chosen and the pagan. The Assyrians used their free will to repent. This shows God displays patience to not only His chosen nation of Israel but also to the pagan nations of the world.

SEVENTY WEEKS PROPHECY

WE SHOULD VIEW PAST EVENTS through the lens of God's word. There are prophetic verses in the Bible that describe how long Israel would exist as a nation. In fact, the entire history of Israel is laid out in stunning detail throughout the scripture. Daniel's prayer and the answer to that prayer (in Daniel chapter nine) provide a stunning revelation about the number of years laid out for Israel's existence as a nation. We can look at this chapter to show an example of how the Bible provided prophecy of every year of Israel's existence as a nation and what their role might be in the final days of the tribulation, especially verses 20-27:

THE SEVENTY "SEVENS"

While I was speaking, praying, and confessing my sin and the sin of my people Israel, and presenting my supplication before Yahweh my God for the holy mountain of my God; yes, while I was speaking in prayer, the man Gabriel, whom I had seen in the vision at the beginning, being caused to fly swiftly, touched me about the time of the evening offering. He instructed me and talked with me, and said, "Daniel, I have now come to give you wisdom and understanding. At the beginning of your petitions the commandment went out, and I have come to tell you; for you are greatly beloved. Therefore, consider the matter, and understand the vision. "Seventy weeks are decreed on your people and on your holy city, to finish disobedience, and to make an end of sins, and to make reconciliation for iniquity, and to bring in everlasting righteousness, and to seal up vision and prophecy, and to anoint the most holy. "Know therefore and discern that from the going out of the commandment to restore and to build Jerusalem to the Anointed One, the prince, will be seven weeks and sixty-two weeks. It will be built again, with street and moat, even in troubled times. After the sixty-two weeks the Anointed One will be cut off, and will have nothing. The people of the prince who come will destroy the city and the sanctuary. Its end will be with a flood, and war will be even to the end. Desolations are

> determined. He will make a firm covenant with many for one week. In the middle of the week he will cause the sacrifice and the offering to cease. On the wing of abominations will come one who makes desolate; and even to the full end, and that determined, wrath will be poured out on the desolate. ~ **Daniel 9: 20-27**

The "seventy weeks" prophecy is one of the most significant and detailed Messianic prophecies of the Old Testament. The chapter begins with Daniel praying for Israel, acknowledging the nation's sins against God, and asking for God's mercy. As Daniel prayed, the angel Gabriel appeared to him and gave him a vision of Israel's future. In verse 24, Gabriel says, "Seventy sevens" are decreed for your people and your holy city." The seventy "sevens" should be understood as seventy "weeks" of years—in other words, a period of 490 years. These verses provide a sort of "clock" which gives an idea of when the Messiah would come and some of the events accompanying His appearance. The prophecy goes on to divide the 490 years into three smaller units: one of 49 years, one of 434 years, and one of seven years. The final "week" of seven years is further divided in half. Verse 25 says, "From the time the word goes out to restore and rebuild Jerusalem until the Anointed One, the ruler, comes, there will be seven 'sevens,' and sixty-two 'sevens.'" Seven "sevens" is 49 years, and sixty-two "sevens" is another 434 years:

49 years + 434 years = 483 years

THE PURPOSE OF THE SEVENTY WEEKS

The prophecy contains a statement concerning God's six-fold purpose in bringing these events to pass. Verse 24 says the purpose is:

- To finish transgression.
- To put an end to sin.
- To atone for wickedness.
- To bring in everlasting righteousness.
- To seal up vision and prophecy.
- To anoint the most holy.

The purpose concerns the total eradication of sin and the establishment of righteousness. The prophecy of the seventy weeks summarizes what happens before Jesus sets up His kingdom here on earth. Notice the third in the list of results: "to atone for wickedness." Jesus accomplished the atonement for sin by His death on the cross (see Romans 3:25).

THE FULFILLMENT OF THE SEVENTY WEEKS

Gabriel said the prophetic clock would start ticking at the time the decree was issued to rebuild Jerusalem. From the date of the decree to the time of the Messiah's appearance would be 483 years. We know from history the command to "restore and rebuild Jerusalem" was given by King Artaxerxes of Persia in 444 B.C. The first unit of 49 years (seven "sevens") covers the time taken to rebuild Jerusalem. Daniel 9:25 says, "Know therefore and discern that from the going out of the commandment to restore and to build Jerusalem to the Anointed One, the prince, will be seven weeks and sixty-two weeks. It will be built again, with street and moat, even in troubled times." (This rebuilding is chronicled in the book of Nehemiah 2:1-8.) Converting the 360-day year used by the ancient Jews, 483 years becomes 476 years on our solar calendar. Adjusting for the switch from B.C. to A.D., 476 years after 444 B.C. places us at A.D. 33, which would coincide with Jesus' triumphal entry into Jerusalem (see Matthew 21:1-9).

The prophecy in Daniel 9 specifies 483 years will elapse after the completion of the temple. After 483 years have passed, "the Anointed One will be cut off." Daniel 9:26 says, "After the sixty-two weeks the Anointed One will be cut off and will have nothing. The people of the prince who come will destroy the city and the sanctuary. Its end will be with a flood, and war will be even to the end. Desolations are determined." Jesus' crucifixion fulfilled the prophecy of the anointed one being cut off. Daniel 9:26 continues with a prediction of "The people of the prince who come will destroy the city and the sanctuary." The prophecy of the destruction of the city and sanctuary was fulfilled with the destruction of Jerusalem in A.D. 70. The "Prince who come" is a reference to the Antichrist, who will have some connection with Rome, since the Romans were responsible for the destruction of Jerusalem.

THE FINAL WEEK OF THE SEVENTY WEEKS

Of the seventy "sevens," sixty-nine have been fulfilled in history. This leaves one more "seven" yet to be fulfilled. Most scholars believe we are now living in a gap between the sixty ninth week and the seventieth week. The prophetic clock is currently paused. The final "seven" of Daniel is what we usually call the tribulation period. Daniel's prophecy reveals some of the actions of the Antichrist, the "ruler who will come."

> He will make a firm covenant with many for one week. In the middle of the week, he will cause the sacrifice and the offering to cease. On the wing of abominations will come one who makes desolate; and even to the full end, and that determined, wrath will be poured out on the desolate. - **Daniel 9:27**

The antichrist will enter a treaty with Israel that will permit them to rebuild the temple and allow sacrifices to be conducted. Israel will rebuild the temple, and sacrifices will be renewed during the first half of the tribulation. Those sacrifices will be permitted during the first half of the tribulation (first three-and-a-half years). After the initial three-and-a-half years the antichrist will bring an end to temple sacrifices and will set up an abomination in the outer courtyard of the temple. Jesus warned of this event:

> When, therefore, you see the abomination of desolation, which was spoken of through Daniel the prophet, standing in the holy place (let the reader understand), then let those who are in Judea flee to the mountains. - **Matthew 24:15-16**

After the Antichrist breaks the covenant with Israel, a time of "Great Tribulation" begins. That time is reserved for the final three-and-a-half years of the tribulation period. Daniel also predicts the Antichrist will face judgment. He only rules "until the end that is decreed is poured out on him." God will only allow evil to go so far. The judgment and punishment the Antichrist will face is certain.

The prophecy of the seventy weeks is complex and amazingly detailed. The prophecy is one of the most studied and written about prophecies in the Bible.[2] The prophecy laid out in stunning detail incredible prophetic details about Israel from the point in time king Artaxerxes gave the decree permitting the city to be rebuilt. In addition, the prophecy foretold the very year Jesus would be crucified for the atonement of our

---

2   "What are the seventy weeks of Daniel?", Got Questions Ministries, *https://www.gotquestions.org/seventy-weeks.html*

sins. What we can learn from these prophetic Bible verses is God is in complete control of history. He foretold, in these Bible verses, the very day Jesus would present himself as the Jewish Messiah and the fact that he would be cut down and crucified for the atonement of your sins.

We are drawing closer to the tribulation period. We are living in a wicked world. I felt writing this book was important to draw Christians closer to God. I pray they would read God's word so they may understand how things might transpire as we progress toward the tribulation period. We will know the antichrist as the individual that enters a treaty to allow Israel to rebuild the temple and permit sacrifices to begin again at the temple. When the antichrist enters a treaty with the nation of Israel, we can be assured we will be getting close to the tribulation period. The seven-year clock will start ticking after the temple has been rebuilt and sacrifices are again permitted.

We should always look for the triumphant return of our Lord:

> I declare the end from the beginning, and from ancient times things that are not yet done. I say: My counsel will stand, and I will do all that I please. ~ **Isaiah 46:10**

> Behold, I come quickly. Blessed is he who keeps the words of the prophecy of this book. ~ **Revelation 22:7**

If you are going to be a good witness to the gospel you need to know God's word. God says man doesn't live by bread alone but by every word of His truth. My prayer for you is you will grow to love God's word as I do. The truth in God's word verifies God's in control of the story. That's important to me. You see, I'm much more comfortable knowing He is in control of the story. We have already shown He is love. He is the very essence of love, and His justice is perfect. Who else would you rather have in control of mankind's story?

SETTING THE STAGE

THERE ARE MANY PROPHECIES THAT were provided to Daniel that help set the stage for what the end times will look like. In this chapter we will analyze Daniel's prophetic verses as they will help provide an understanding of what we can expect to take place as we progress toward the end times. Previously in this book we looked at Daniel chapter 2. That prophecy centered around the dream that king Nebuchadnezzar had and included Daniel's interpretation of the dream. The vision presented to king Nebuchadnezzar, and Daniel's interpretation of the dream provide evidence of God's sovereignty over the nations of the earth. This chapter also provides evidence for how God has set the stage for the alignment of nations as we approach the end times.

As we will recall from earlier, Daniel's interpretation of the dream predicted, in astonishing detail, the rise and fall of the following kingdoms:

- The Babylonian empire
- The Medes and Persian empires
- Greece
- The Roman Empire
- A kingdom yet to rise (this will be the kingdom the antichrist reigns over)
- The kingdom of Jesus (ushered in by the stone striking the feet of the statue)[3]

Beyond seeing God's authority being displayed over the nations we can glean a few additional details in analyzing these Bible verses that speak to how events might unfold as we move toward the end times and the kingdom the antichrist will reign over. By analyzing what we see in the statue presented to King Nebuchadnezzar we can comment on a few observations:[4]

- The dream shows clear de-evolution of the kingdoms as we

---

[3] "What is the meaning of Nebuchadnezzar's dream in Daniel 2?", Got Questions Ministries, *https://www.gotquestions.org/Nebuchadnezzars-dream.html*

[4] "Will Jesus come back", AboutIslam, *https://aboutislam.net/counseling/ask-about-islam/will-jesus-come-back/*

progress toward the kingdom the antichrist will preside over. This very clearly depicts the de-evolution of humanity and of its temporal power always going down, always less valuable, and ultimately dissipated so that nothing is left of it. We can see this represented in the dream in that as we move down from head to toe the materials that make up that portion of the statue become less and less valuable.

- We come to the legs of iron, the fourth empire which is Rome. The fact that there are two legs provide details that there's going to be some kind of division. This is very significant because of its interpretation. The Roman Empire came into being as one but in the fourth century it was split into two, western empire and eastern empire, in the time of Constantine. The capital of the western empire was Rome, the capital of the eastern empire was Constantinople. We can see this split represented in the vision of the status as we see two legs. This is important because ultimately the leader of the antichrist's kingdom will come out of one of these legs.

The above dream from King Nebuchadnezzar helps us understand when the kingdom of the antichrist might come into existence. There must be four major kingdoms that come prior to it. Those four kingdoms are Babylon, the Medes and Persian empire, Greece, and the Roman empire. All four of those kingdoms have since come into existence. As a result, we can see now we are living in the time just prior to the emergence of a future kingdom that will arise on the world stage. This new kingdom will be the kingdom the antichrist will preside over. Daniel provides additional clues in Daniel chapter 8 about where the kingdom of the antichrist might arise.

DANIEL CHAPTER 8:

In the third year of the reign of king Belshazzar, a vision appeared to me, even to me, Daniel, after that which appeared to me at the first. I saw the vision. Now it was so, that when I saw, I was in the citadel of Susa, which is in the province of Elam. I saw in the vision, and I was by the river Ulai. Then I lifted up my eyes, and saw, and behold, there stood before the river a ram which had two horns. The two horns were high; but one was higher than the other, and the higher came up last. I saw the ram pushing westward, northward, and southward. No animals could stand before him. There wasn't any who could deliver out of his hand; but he did according to his will, and magnified himself. As I was considering, behold, a male goat came from the west over the surface of the whole earth, and didn't touch the ground. The goat had a notable horn between his eyes. He came to the ram that had the two horns, which I saw standing before the river, and ran on him in the fury of his power. I saw him come close to the ram, and he was moved with anger against him, and struck the ram, and broke his two horns. There was no power in the ram to stand before him; but he cast him down to the ground, and trampled on him. There was no one who could deliver the ram out of his hand. The male goat magnified himself exceedingly. When he was strong, the great horn was broken; and instead of it there came up four notable horns toward the four winds of the sky. Out of one of them came out a little horn, which grew exceedingly great, toward the south, and toward the east, and toward the glorious land. It grew great, even to the army of the sky; and it cast down some of the army and of the stars to the ground and trampled on them. Yes, it magnified itself, even to the prince of the army; and it took away from him the continual burnt offering, and the place of his sanctuary was cast down. The army was given over to it together with the continual burnt offering through disobedience. It cast down truth to the ground, and it did its pleasure and prospered. Then I heard a holy one speaking; and another holy one said to that certain one who spoke, "How long will the vision about the continual burnt offering, and the disobedience that makes desolate, to give both the sanctuary and the army to be trodden under foot be?" He said to me, "To two thousand and three hundred evenings and mornings. Then the sanctuary will be cleansed." When I, even I Daniel, had seen the vision, I sought to understand it. Then behold, there stood before me something like the appearance of a man. I heard a man's voice between the banks of the Ulai, which called, and said, "Gabriel, make this man understand the vision." So he came near where I stood; and when he came, I was frightened, and fell on my face; but he said to me, "Understand, son of man; for the vision belongs to the time of the end." Now as he was speaking with me, I fell into a deep sleep with my face toward the ground; but he touched me, and set me upright. He said, "Behold, I will make you know what will be in the latter time of the indignation; for it belongs to the appointed time of the end. The ram which you saw, that had the two horns, they are the kings of Media and Persia. The rough male goat is the king of Greece. The great horn that is between his eyes is the first king. As for that which was broken, in the place where four stood up, four kingdoms will stand up out of the nation, but not with his power. "In the latter time of their kingdom, when the transgressors have come to the full, a king of fierce face, and understanding dark sentences, will stand up. His power will be mighty, but not by his own power. He will destroy awesomely, and will prosper in what he does. He will destroy the mighty ones and the holy people. Through his policy he will cause deceit to prosper in his hand. He will magnify himself in his heart, and he will destroy many in their security. He will also stand up against the prince of princes; but he will be broken without hand. "The vision of the evenings and mornings which has been told is true; but seal up the vision, for it belongs to many days to come." I, Daniel, fainted, and was sick for some days. Then I rose up, and did the king's business. I wondered at the vision, but no one understood it.

We learn from study of these Bible verses that it was Alexander the Great who broke through and changed the whole world system. Out of Alexander there came four lesser empires. History makes clear who those four empires were. They included Macedon (Which is northern Greece under Antigonus), Pergamum (Turkey under the Attalids), Syria (Under the Seleucids), and Egypt (Under the Ptolemies). Daniel 8:9-11 communicates that the antichrist will arise out of one of these empires during the end times. Much of the purpose of Daniel 7 and 8 is to tell us about the antichrist. But in each case, it gives us a historical background and a geographical background against which we can assess the information. It says in Daniel 8:9-11 out of one of them came a little horn which grew exceedingly great toward the south, toward the east, and toward the glorious land. It grew up to the host of heaven and it cast down some of the host and some of the stars to the ground and trampled them. He even exalted himself as high as the prince of the host. This is clearly the antichrist who eventually sets himself on the level of Jesus. The question we must ask ourselves is which of these four kingdoms can we expect the antichrist to come out of. It says in Daniel 8:9 that "it became exceeding great toward the south, toward the east, and toward the glorious land." The south is Egypt, the east is Syria, and the glorious land is the land of Israel. The nearest place from which the power could arise would seem to be Turkey, so one might expect the antichrist to come out of Turkey based upon this interpretation of Daniel chapter 8.[5]

The Bible provides another clue that the antichrist might arise out of Turkey. In Revelation chapter 2 the Bible speaks to one of the seven churches in Asia. This church was in a city called Pergamum. Pergamum resides in Turkey, and you can see from this Bible verse that God identifies that city to be where the throne of Satan is located.

DANIEL 2:12-17

To the angel of the assembly in Pergamum write: He who has the sharp two-edged sword says these things: "I know your works and where you dwell, **where Satan's throne is**. You hold firmly to my name, and didn't deny my faith in the days of Antipas my witness, my faithful one, who was killed among you, **where Satan dwells**. But I have a few things against you, because you have there some who hold the teaching of Balaam, who taught Balak to throw a stumbling block before the children of Israel, to eat things sacrificed to idols, and to commit sexual immorality. So you also have some who hold to the teaching of the Nicolaitans likewise. Repent therefore, or else I am coming to you quickly, and I will make war against them with the sword of my mouth. He who has an ear, let him hear what the Spirit says to the assemblies. To him who overcomes, to him I will give of the hidden manna, and I will give him a white stone, and on the stone a new name written, which no one knows but he who receives it.

---

[5] https://aboutislam.net/counseling/ask-about-islam/will-jesus-come-back/

This Bible verse also contains visions of Jesus having the double-edged sword and doing battle with the double-edged sword that comes from His mouth. This harkens us directly to the last days where Jesus says He will defeat Satan's army using the double-edged sword that comes from His mouth, so these Bible verses seem to point toward the end of times. Note the double-edged sword here is an important detail. Jesus is said to have a double-edged sword. This sword represents His truth, which is represented as His word. The two edges are significant as each edge represents a Biblical covenant (the old and new covenant of the Bible). The fact that both edges are on the same sword is also significant, it means the truth of God's holy word is only complete when taking both the new and the old covenant together. That is only found within the truths of Christianity! This is another important detail Christians should remember as we approach the final days to help us avoid any deceptions that might be conveyed to us during those times by other competing messages we might hear.

Daniel's prayer, and answer to his prayer in chapter nine of Daniel provide other details about Israel's role to play in the end times as well as additional details about how we might be able to recognize the antichrist. Daniel's prayer and the answer to that prayer was provided in the previous chapter of this book (Israel's 70-week prophecy). As we recall that prophecy provide stunning details about Israel's role in bringing forth the Messiah as it provides the exact timing of when the Messiah would present himself in Israel and when He would be struck down for the atonement of your sins. This prophecy also provides evidence regarding Israel's position and the role they will play in the end times. Amazingly, this chapter reveals that Israel must exist as a nation in the end times because a treaty would be signed between the nation of Israel and the antichrist during the end times. I say this is amazing because Israel only re-emerged as a sovereign nation in modern times. As a result, I think it's become increasingly evident that we are living in the end times and God is, in fact, in control of the events that have taken place and will continue to take place as we progress down this path. As we recall from our previous study of Daniel's 70-week prophecy the Bible provided the six-fold purpose for bringing these events to pass as follows:

- To finish transgression.
- To put an end to sin.
- To atone for wickedness.
- To bring in everlasting righteousness.

- To seal up vision and prophecy.
- To anoint the most holy.

The purpose of the prophecy has some incredibly important details that we, as Christians, must be aware of. It is clearly stated, through this prophecy God would put an end to sin and atone for wickedness. This speaks to the fact that Jesus would be the sacrificial lamb. Through the perfect sacrifice He made on the cross your sins are forgiven. It is also clearly stated it would bring in everlasting righteousness and anoint the most holy. This was done upon the resurrection of Jesus. Jesus is still alive and resides with God. He will return and rule as your righteous king. He will bring in everlasting righteousness. That is only possible by the fact that he was dead and was raised by God after His death on the cross for the atonement of your sins. There is a final detail contained here which is incredibly important for Christians. That final detail states that, through this prophecy, God would "seal up vision and prophecy". This verifies for us in God's holy word that Jesus would be the last prophet. There would be no prophet sent after Jesus. This is incredibly important because the Islamic faith recognizes Jesus as a prophet, but they don't recognize him as the *last* prophet. They recognize Mohammad as the last prophet. They also don't believe Jesus died on the cross for the atonement of your sins. Islam doesn't believe God needs a son, and they don't recognize the death and resurrection of Jesus. Islam teaches Jesus' death on the cross was only meant to look like He died on the cross, but they believe God took Him up to heaven before he died, and He resides with God and is waiting for a time when He will come back to earth as the return of a great prophet in the end times. Islam believes the purpose Jesus will be sent back to earth in the end times will be to correct the misconceptions Christians have about God's word. They say he will correct the Christians. He will communicate to them that He never died, and He was never resurrected by God. This is part of the great deception that will arise during the end times that will seek to lead even the elect away from God and His holy word. It's very important for Christian's to understand this will be a lie, but it will be presented as truth during the end times to the entire world, and will be presented with many miraculous signs such as the False prophet bringing fire down from heaven

God has chosen to use the nation of Israel to set the stage for what will take place during the end times. In addition, God provides, within the pages of the Bible, many promises made to Israel and provides details about how the nation of Israel would be used to bless the world by bringing Jesus Christ (the Messiah) out of Israel to become a true blessing to the world. The Bible provides in stunning detail the promises made to Israel and communicates prophetic events that have taken place in Israel's history that have shaped the world as we know it today. What we can see within the pages of the Bible is God has used Israel to set the world stage for the final days, and it will be upon this stage (within the Holy Lands) that the final chapters of humanity will take place.

SEVEN CHURCHES

WE SHOULD VIEW EVERYTHING THROUGH the lens of God's word. His word is truth. It never changes. The Bible should be used as the steady compass to guide us in every decision. The Bible says we should meditate on the word of God.

> Blessed is the man who doesn't walk in the counsel of the wicked, nor stand on the path of sinners, nor sit in the seat of scoffers; but his delight is in Yahweh's law. On his law he meditates day and night." ~ **Psalms 1:1-2**

We are not simply to read the word of God. God desires that we meditate on His word and to act on His word. Many translations of the Bible use the word ruminate in place of meditate. The word ruminate comes from the Latin word *ruminatus*. The word means to "chew the cud" as a cow chews the cud. The cow chews, swallows, brings the cud up again, and chews the cud again to get all the nutrients possible out of the cud. Such is the picture painted regarding how we are to study and meditate on the word of God. God's word should be the lens to draw meaning from everything in our lives. We should use His word to make decisions about everything we are faced with. As we walk through the pages of the book of Revelation it's important to try to understand what the book is telling us. Revelation can be a difficult book to comprehend but we must try to glean the meaning that God wants us to understand from the book. We will begin walking through the book of Revelation in Chapter 1 as we examine the message Jesus wanted to provide to His churches.

The book of Revelation is direct testimony from Jesus (being provided to John, His disciple). Verse seven and eight provide a prophetic vision of the second coming of Jesus. They speak to Jesus' promise to return. In verses four and five He speaks of the fact that He is alive. He speaks of His deity and authority to provide this message to the churches. In verse eleven, John is asked to write down what he sees, what is now and what will take place later. Verses twelve through sixteen paint a picture of John in his vision seeing seven lampstands (lampstands typically represent a spiritual message or a church). John sees seven stars (stars typically represent angels). What John is seeing here is the angels representing each of the seven churches. Finally, John sees Jesus himself, the Son of Man. The sight of Jesus in His resurrected body overwhelms John to the point he immediately falls at the feet of Jesus as though he were dead. These verses illustrate why we can trust His promise (because He is the Alpha and Omega). Jesus dictates seven letters to seven churches in Asia Minor. Jesus' testimony is being sent directly to these seven churches. In these seven letters Jesus critiques how these churches have been conducting themselves.

One thing I find interesting in these chapters is the very sight of Jesus in His resurrected body was so overwhelming to John that he couldn't take everything in without falling at His feet like a dead man. Seeing John laying there at His feet Jesus touches him and says, "Do not be afraid." This is simply awesome! John's vision of Jesus in his resurrected body was too much for him to take in. It overwhelmed John to the point of death. Jesus' reaction to seeing John laying (as if he were dead) at His feet is simply to touch John and tell him not to be afraid. I have always been in fear about what is going to happen when we come face to face with our living God. It's going to be terrifying. The picture painted here in God's word tells us what will take place. We are going to come face to face with Jesus. We are going to be overwhelmed. We are going to be so overcome with fear and awe we will fall at His feet as if we were dead. Jesus, who is love, is going to touch us. He's going to encourage us to take heart. The very first thing He's going to say to His believers is "Don't be afraid!." The picture being painted here is of a loving and merciful God. Jesus goes on in the rest of the chapter to communicate to John exactly who He is, tells John to write down what he sees, and explains what John is seeing to him.

Revelation chapters 2 and 3 walk us through the message to these seven churches. These letters are so important we should take a moment and read *all* of chapters two and three:

REVELATION CHAPTER 2

To the angel of the assembly in Ephesus write: "He who holds the seven stars in his right hand, he who walks among the seven golden lamp stands says these things. "I know your works, and your toil and perseverance, and that you can't tolerate evil men, and have tested those who call themselves apostles, and they are not, and found them false. You have perseverance and have endured for my name's sake and have not grown weary. But

I have this against you, that you left your first love. Remember therefore from where you have fallen, and repent and do the first works; or else I am coming to you swiftly and will move your lamp stand out of its place, unless you repent. But this you have, that you hate the works of the Nicolaitans, which I also hate. He who has an ear, let him hear what the Spirit says to the assemblies. To him who overcomes I will give to eat from the tree of life, which is in the Paradise of my God.

"To the angel of the assembly in Smyrna write: "The first and the last, who was dead, and has come to life says these things: "I know your works, oppression, and your poverty (but you are rich), and the blasphemy of those who say they are Jews, and they are not, but are a synagogue of Satan. Don't be afraid of the things which you are about to suffer. Behold, the devil is about to throw some of you into prison, that you may be tested; and you will have oppression for ten days. Be faithful to death, and I will give you the crown of life. He who has an ear, let him hear what the Spirit says to the assemblies. He who overcomes won't be harmed by the second death.

"To the angel of the assembly in Pergamum write: "He who has the sharp two-edged sword says these things: "I know your works and where you dwell, where Satan's throne is. You hold firmly to my name, and didn't deny my faith in the days of Antipas my witness, my faithful one, who was killed among you, where Satan dwells. But I have a few things against you, because you have there some who hold the teaching of Balaam, who taught Balak to throw a stumbling block before the children of Israel, to eat things sacrificed to idols, and to commit sexual immorality. So you also have some who hold to the teaching of the Nicolaitans likewise. Repent therefore, or else I am coming to you quickly, and I will make war against them with the sword of my mouth. He who has an ear, let him hear what the Spirit says to the assemblies. To him who overcomes, to him I will give of the hidden manna, and I will give him a white stone, and on the stone a new name written, which no one knows but he who receives it.

To the angel of the assembly in Thyatira write: "The Son of God, who has his eyes like a flame of fire, and his feet are like burnished brass, says these things: "I know your works, your love, faith, service, patient endurance, and that your last works are more than the first. But I have this against you, that you tolerate your woman, Jezebel, who calls herself a prophetess. She teaches and seduces my servants to commit sexual immorality, and to eat things sacrificed to idols. I gave her time to repent, but she refuses to repent of her sexual immorality. Behold, I will throw her and those who commit adultery with her into a bed of great oppression, unless they repent of her works. I will kill her children with Death, and all the assemblies will know that I am he who searches the minds and hearts. I will give to each one of you according to your deeds. But to you I say, to the rest who are in Thyatira, as many as don't have this teaching, who don't know what some call 'the deep things of Satan,' to you I say, I am not putting any other burden on you. Nevertheless, hold that which you have firmly until I come. He who overcomes, and he who keeps my works to the end, to him I will give authority over the nations. He will rule them with a rod of iron, shattering them like clay pots; as I also have received of my Father: and I will give him the morning star. He who has an ear, let him hear what the Spirit says to the assemblies.

REVELATION CHAPTER 3

And to the angel of the assembly in Sardis write: "He who has the seven Spirits of God and the seven stars says these things: "I know your works, that you have a reputation of being alive, but you are dead. Wake up and keep the things that remain, which you were about to throw away, for I have found no works of yours perfected before my God. Remember therefore how you have received and heard. Keep it and repent. If therefore you won't watch, I will come as a thief, and you won't know what hour I will come upon you. Nevertheless, you have a few names in Sardis that didn't defile their garments. They will walk with me in white, for they are worthy. He who overcomes will be arrayed in white garments, and I will in no way blot his name out of the book of life, and I will confess his name before my Father, and before his angels. He who has an ear, let him hear what the Spirit says to the assemblies.

"To the angel of the assembly in Philadelphia write: "He who is holy, he who is true, he who has the key of David, he who opens and no one can shut, and who shuts and no one opens, says these things: "I know your works (behold, I have set before you an open door, which no one can shut), that you have a little power, and kept my word, and didn't deny my name. Behold, I give some of the synagogue of Satan, of those who say they are Jews, and they are not, but lie—behold, I will make them to come and worship before your feet, and to know that I have loved you. Because you kept my command to endure, I also will keep you from the hour of testing which is to come on the whole world, to test those who dwell on the earth. I am coming quickly! Hold firmly that which you have, so that no one takes your crown. He who overcomes, I will make him a pillar in the temple of my God, and he will go out from there no more. I will write on him the name of my God and the name of the city of my God, the new Jerusalem, which comes down out of heaven from my God, and my own new name. He who has an ear, let him hear what the Spirit says to the assemblies.

To the angel of the assembly in Laodicea write: "The Amen, the Faithful and True Witness, the Beginning of God's creation, says these things: "I know your works, that you are neither cold nor hot. I wish you were cold or hot. So, because you are lukewarm, and neither hot nor cold, I will vomit you out of my mouth. Because you say, 'I am rich, and have gotten riches, and have need of nothing;' and don't know that you are the wretched one, miserable, poor, blind, and naked; I counsel you to buy from me gold refined by fire, that you may become rich; and white garments, that you may clothe yourself, and that the shame of your nakedness may not be revealed; and eye salve to anoint your eyes, that you may see. As many as I love, I reprove and chasten. Be zealous therefore, and repent. Behold, I stand at the door and knock. If anyone hears my voice and opens the door, then I will come in to him, and will dine with him, and he with me. He who overcomes, I will give to him to sit down with me on my throne, as I also overcame, and sat down with my Father on his throne. He who has an ear, let him hear what the Spirit says to the assemblies.

Whenever we hear something like "Whoever has ears, let them hear," we should be paying close attention! These messages are being provided to all Christian churches. These verses provide insight and warnings about who Jesus is and how these churches should conduct themselves. These verses communicate a few key attributes of Jesus as follows:

- Jesus holds the seven stars in His right hand and walks among the seven golden lampstands. (Jesus actively walks amongst His churches and is sovereign over the angels in heaven).
- Jesus is the first and the last (He is omniscient).
- Jesus died and came to life again (this speaks of Jesus death and resurrection).
- Jesus has the sharp, double-edged sword which represents His word (Jesus has the word of truth being the combined Old and New Testaments).
- Jesus' eyes are like blazing fire and His feet are like burnished bronze (provides a description of Jesus in His resurrected body).
- Jesus holds the seven spirits of God and the seven stars (Jesus is sovereign over angels).
- Jesus is holy and true; He holds the key of David. What He opens no one can shut, and what He shuts no one can open (Jesus has the keys to salvation).
- Jesus is the Amen (the final word), the faithful and true witness and the ruler of God's creation.

These verses also provide information about what Jesus expects from His churches, how they are to conduct themselves. The verses warn against the following:

- False doctrines.
- Being on guard against false prophets within the church (Toleration of the woman Jezebel, who calls herself a prophetess).
- Dabbling in the occult.

- Marrying non-believers (holding to the teaching of Balaam).
- Eating food sacrificed to other gods.
- Sexual immorality within the church.
- Turning cold (losing your fire for God's message).
- Acquiring too much worldly wealth.
- Feeling you have no need to rely upon God.

These warnings are meant to inspire Christians to always be ready for the return of Jesus. You do not know at what day, nor what hour He will return. You also do not know what time God might decide to call you home to be with Him, so be ready. These verses provide the following amazing promises from God.

- The victor will be provided the right to eat from the Tree of Life (eternal life), which is in God's paradise.
- The crown of life (the glory of eternal life).
- The victor will never be harmed by the second death.
- The victor will be provided with some of the hidden manna. I believe this may signify hidden truths in the Bible because God's word is what real believers are said to feed upon.
- The victor will be provided with a white stone. A new name will be inscribed on the stone. No one will know the name except the one who receives it.
- Jesus will give to each of you according to your works. God's rewards in Heaven for believers whose names are written in the book of life will be provided based upon their works performed here on earth. We must understand salvation is through faith alone. Works do not get us into heaven, but there will be rewards in heaven based upon the works we have performed here on earth serving God.
- Give him authority over the nations (believers will judge the nations in God's new kingdom).
- Give him the morning star (which may represent Jesus Himself.).
- To walk with Jesus dressed in white, for they are deemed worthy.
- Will never blot their names out of the lamb's book of life but will acknowledge their name before His Father and His angels (This speaks to the fact that once someone is saved their name can never be blotted out of the lamb's book of life. Their salvation is secure).

I have always been curious what the white stone represented in the above set of promises. In researching what the white stone might represent I found this appears to be a promise of intimacy with God. Research I have conducted says it was customary in Jesus' day for guests invited to a dinner to have a white stone placed at their seat with their name on it. The white stone accomplished two things. First, it marked the guest's seat at the table. Second, it offered an intimate thought to each guest from the host. When the guests were seated, they could look at the white stone and underneath would be a private message to them from the host. It was a way for the host to share an intimate message with his guests.[6] It appears the Lord's promises He will reveal Himself in a personal and intimate way. Isn't it amazing God Almighty, the creator of the universe, would want to reveal Himself to you in a personal and intimate way? To me this is simply amazing. How blessed we are to serve a God whose very nature is love and who desires to have an intimate relationship with us.

Within chapter 3 of the book of Revelation God provides a very specific promise to the church of Philadelphia. Revelation 3:10 says, "Because you kept my command to endure, I also will keep you from the hour of testing, which is to come on the whole world, to test those who dwell on the earth." I believe this is a direct promise from God that He will protect His true believers during the time of the great tribulation. As I have said previously in this book, God makes a distinction between His followers and those that don't follow Him. I believe this is a direct promise from God that he will keep, nourish, and protect His true believers during the tribulation period because the hour of testing is speaking directly to that time of trial that will be experienced on the whole world. I believe this is the hour of trial know to Christians as the great tribulation period as spoken about in the book of Revelation. True Christians, true followers of Christ, will be protected from the many plagues God is unleashing upon the world during this time of great trial. Those plagues are meant to call the unbelieving people of the world to repentance and get them to repent and return to their one true God. They are not meant to cause suffering for the true believers in faith that will be living on the earth at that time. God has promised in this verse to keep His true believers protected during these times of great trial.

---

[6]   Rev. J. Patrick Street, "Pastor Column: I will give him a white stone", <u>Marion Star</u>, February 18, 2022 <u>https://www.marionstar.com/story/news/2022/02/18/pastor-column-meaning-behind-gift-white-stone/6752034001/</u>

In his letter to the Ephesians (6:10-18), the Apostle Paul tells us to take up the "full armor of God." The battle we fight is one of a spiritual nature. The prize of the battle is to win as many human souls as possible to either salvation or damnation. Let that reality sink in: do you feel valued knowing there is spiritual warfare being waged for your soul? War has been raging since the very creation of the universe. God's word tells us to fight this spiritual battle with the tools He equips us with. I encourage everyone reading this book to take hold of everything God equips you with. We are to actively participate in the battle for these human souls. If you choose to sit on the sidelines, you are doing Satan's work. If you decide not to participate in this battle, Satan doesn't need to bother with you. You make the choice using your own free will. Nobody can make the choice for you.

These Bible verses reveal the following for us:

- The Bible gives us guidance for how we are to act as the body of Christ when we witness to non-believers.
- The Bible promises rewards in Heaven if we make the choice to participate by actively witnessing to non-believers.

I pray everyone reading this book will make the same choice I have made. To bend the knee and accept Jesus as their lord and savior. To know He alone can take the penalty of your sin. Jesus completed this on the cross when He became a perfect sacrifice for the atonement of your sin. God's desired to be with you from the very beginning of creation. He wants nothing more than to draw you back to Him. I pray you would also consider what the word "works" means. The word "works" represent rewards for actively participating in God's kingdom to save as many souls as possible before Jesus returns to earth in His second coming. Finally, I pray everyone reading this book would realize God created everything with its own free will. I pray you will use your free will to decide to participate in this battle for the remaining lost human souls.

God is love. He shows in the book of Revelation examples of how He expects His churches to conduct themselves. He provides examples from the seven churches so we can examine our own church to see if we are serving in the way He expects. If we see things that need to be corrected in our church, we should lovingly seek to make corrections so the lamp we shine into the world is as bright and loving as possible. God desires our churches to be on fire for Him. He expects us to be His hands and feet to carry His message of good news to the world. Let us examine our church so we will be able to make any necessary corrections. We should work in a loving way for His people. He expects us to reflect His nature. We are to reflect love to the church we have chosen to be a part of as we work to spread His gospel to those souls currently lost.

OPENING THE SEALS

THE BOOK OF REVELATION PROVIDES information about opening the seven seals. These Bible verses provide information about what we, as believers, can expect to happen in the final days. Jesus is the sole entity with the authority to open these seals, and He revealed the meaning of these seals to his apostle John as documented in the book of Revelation.

Prior to the Bible verses concerning the opening of the seven seals John is said to be openly weeping. He is weeping because he fears no one may be found worthy of opening the seals. If this is the case, the meaning of what is contained within the scrolls can't be revealed. John begins by describing the seals in chapter five:

> I saw, in the right hand of him who sat on the throne, a book written inside and outside, sealed shut with seven seals. I saw a mighty angel proclaiming with a loud voice, "Who is worthy to open the book, and to break its seals?" No one in heaven above, or on the earth, or under the earth, was able to open the book or to look in it. **Then I wept much, because no one was found worthy to open the book or to look in it**. One of the elders said to me, "Don't weep. Behold, the Lion who is of the tribe of Judah, the Root of David, has overcome: he who opens the book and its seven seals." ~ **Revelation 5:1-7**

We see only one entity found worthy to open the seals and read from the scroll. The lone entity is Jesus, the lamb of God. He alone is found worthy because He alone laid down His life as a sacrificial atonement for our sins. Jesus alone sanctifies human souls; thus, He alone is found worthy to open these seals and decipher what is written within the scroll. The fact Jesus is unique in the authority to open the seals represents He also is uniquely qualified to address questions you might have along your path of ministry. The mystery of the seals (questions answered) includes what is going to happen during the end times. Jesus chose to deliver some details to John about how the end times will unfold. It is important for us to understand what Jesus is saying as we are participating in the end time ministry. Let's look at the information Jesus chose to provide about the meaning of each seal as they are opened.

THE FIRST SEAL:

> Then a white horse appeared, and he who sat on it had a bow. A crown was given to him, and he came out conquering, and to conquer. - **Revelation 6:2**

In the first seal we see a rider on a white horse. The rider on the horse is the antichrist. The rider is mounted on a white horse. The color white represents peace because the antichrist will rise to power by promising peace. This first seal is opened at the beginning of the tribulation. The first three-and-a-half years of the tribulation will be marked by an appearance of peace, but the antichrist will ultimately bring war and destruction in the final three-and-a-half years of the tribulation period.[7] The weapon the rider carries is a bow. The bow typically represents some sort of offensive weapon in the Bible. Jesus is depicted as having a double-edged sword coming out of His mouth when He returns to earth. The double-edged sword represents truth, which is His word. The tool Jesus uses to defeat Satan and those attached to the world is simply speaking the truth of His word. The rider, depicted with a bow, comes with an offensive weapon. The tool he will use to try to convince people to come to him is an offensive weapon (pressure, manipulation, and coercion in a menacing way). We can be assured anyone coming to us in this type of manner is only trying to deceive us.

The rider on this horse is representative of the antichrist. He will arrive with promises of peace and prosperity, but his message will be a false message and will be delivered in a coercive and manipulative way. The rider emerging from the first seal also signifies false gospels and false religions. False religious principles have caused many to be persecuted in the name of religion. Anyone that fails to recognize Jesus' ministry, death by crucifixion, and resurrection can be considered to have the spirit of the antichrist in them.

---

[7] Roger Barrier, "Opening the Seven Seals of Revelation", Preach It Teach It, September 10, 2021, *Gog and Magog: A Revelation from John Explained - Preach It Teach It*

THE SECOND SEAL:

> When he opened the second seal, I heard the second living creature saying, "Come!" Another came out: a red horse. To him who sat on it was given power to take peace from the earth, and that they should kill one another. There was given to him a great sword. ~ **Revelation 6:3-4**

The meaning of the second seal is pointing to war on earth. The rider of this seal will take peace from the earth. This will take place during the second half of the tribulation period when the antichrist sets up his image at the temple of God and demands to be worshiped.[8] The antichrist will stop all sacrifices at the temple and will declare war on anyone that refuses to worship him on earth. We have seen wars historically and will continue to see them through the end of days. This rider carries a great sword. The wielder of this sword carries false truths with him, as the sword is not specified to be a double-edged sword. This rider will try to coerce, compel, and manipulate people into following a false truth.

We can see a historic representation of the second seal by looking at wars fought in the past. Each war has had its own amount of barbarism and bloodshed. The nations participating in the wars each have their own part to play in the death associated with each war. The color of the horse coming out of the second seal is red. The red horse of bloodshed. Red represents the great bloodshed seen in past wars and ongoing bloodshed we will continue to see in future wars. Red also represents the blood of the martyrs that has been shed throughout history.

THE THIRD SEAL:

> When he opened the third seal, I heard the third living creature saying, "Come and see!" And behold, a black horse, and he who sat on it had a balance in his hand. I heard a voice in the middle of the four living creatures saying, "A choenix of wheat for a denarius, and three choenix of barley for a denarius! Don't damage the oil and the wine!" ~ **Revelation 6: 5-6**

---

8   Roger Barrier, "Opening the Seven Seals of Revelation", Preach It Teach It, September 10, 2021, *Gog and Magog: A Revelation from John Explained - Preach It Teach It*

The picture of a black horse represents famine. During this famine it will take an entire day's wages just to purchase a quart of wheat. I believe there will also be a famine of God's word at this time of the Great Tribulation as the antichrist will seek to destroy all copies of God's word. It should be noted famine on earth is caused because we fail to follow the pure and truthful precepts laid out in God's word. If we all chose to follow the two most important commandments to love God with all your heart and love your neighbor as yourself, we would have no hunger in the world because we would naturally care for each other. We would feed and provide clothing for the needy if we all followed God's precepts.

THE FOURTH SEAL:

> When he opened the fourth seal, I heard the fourth living creature saying, "Come and see!" And behold, a pale horse, and the name of he who sat on it was Death. Hades followed with him. Authority over one fourth of the earth, to kill with the sword, with famine, with death, and by the wild animals of the earth was given to him." ~ **Revelation 6: 7-8**

The breaking of this seal represents death. The natural result of war and famine is death. The Greek word "pale" describes the ashen look of a dead body without blood. The Bible states one fourth of the Earth's population will die because of war and subsequent famine that are unleashed by the breaking of the first two seals.[9]

THE 5TH SEAL:

> When he opened the fifth seal, I saw underneath the altar the souls of those who had been killed for the Word of God, and for the testimony of the Lamb which they had. They cried with a loud voice, saying, "How long, Master, the holy and true, until you judge and avenge our blood on those who dwell on the earth?" A long white robe was given to each of them. They were told that they should rest yet for a while, until their fellow ser-

---

[9]   Roger Barrier, "Opening the Seven Seals of Revelation", Preach It Teach it, September 10, 2021, *Gog and Magog: A Revelation from John Explained - Preach It Teach It*

vants and their brothers, who would also be killed even as they were, should complete their course." ~ **Revelation 6:9-11**

The altar represents the earth. The blood shed from the martyr's testimony is crying out to God. Their blood cries out to God like Abel's blood cried out to God after Cain, his brother, murdered him. For those who say the very nature of man is good, I would challenge you with this Biblical truth. The very first capital crime was committed by the son of the first husband and wife God created. Once man sinned evil entered the world. Sin continues to work to tear the world apart to this very day. The fact is God tells us no man is perfect in this current age. Some of us are better than others, but let's face facts: nobody's perfect, so let's not assume man's very nature is good. I would argue we're closer to man's very nature in this current age to be self-centered and evil. The Bible supports this view in Romans 3:10: As it is written, "**There is no one righteous; no, not one.**" *[emphasis added]* Mankind left on its own, without the guidance of God's perfect word will get lost. Ultimately destruction will follow.

The souls represented in the breaking of the fifth seal are those who have been martyred for their great loyalty to Jesus. The altar is a place of sacrifice and death. These saints are right where their blood was poured out. These martyred souls are crying out to God and asking for God's vengeance on their murderers. These martyred souls are provided long, flowing robes by Jesus and told to "Rest a little while longer." They are rewarded and honored by Jesus for dying the ultimate death. The Lord then says, "Wait until the full number of martyr's is complete." What Jesus is saying here is there are still some yet to be martyred during the Great Tribulation.[10]

THE 6TH SEAL:

I saw when he opened the sixth seal, and there was a great earthquake. The sun became black as sackcloth made of hair, and the whole moon became as blood. The stars of the sky fell to the earth, like a fig tree dropping its unripe figs when it is shaken by a great wind. The sky was removed like a scroll when its rolled

---

[10] Roger Barrier, "Opening the Seven Seals of Revelation", Preach It Teach It, September 10, 2021, *Gog and Magog: A Revelation from John Explained - Preach It Teach It*

up. Every mountain and island was moved out of its place. The
kings of the earth, the princes, the commanding officers, the
rich, the strong, and every slave and free person hid themselves
in the caves and in the rocks of the mountains. They called to
the mountains and the rocks, "Fall on us and hide us from the
face of him who sits on the throne and from the wrath of the
Lamb! For the great day of their wrath has come, and who can
withstand it?" ~ **Revelation 6:12-17**

The opening of the sixth seal presents God's use of natural forces to
gain our attention. God uses natural forces such as earthquakes and signs
within the celestial bodies to gain our attention. The breaking of this seal
also includes a prophecy of the second coming of Jesus at the very end of
the Great Tribulation.

THE OPENING OF THE 7TH SEAL:

When he opened the seventh seal, there was silence in heaven for
about half an hour. I saw the seven angels who stand before God,
and seven trumpets were given to them. ~ **Revelation 8: 1-2**

The opening of the seventh seal marks a second wave of judgments.
One thing to note is there is a pause for a period here before the next set
of judgments in Revelation. This silence in heaven represents a waiting
period of deep contemplation. This silence in heaven is meant to signify
God's mercy towards humanity.

It's a blessing Jesus has been found worthy to open the seals in the
book of Revelation. God is love. Jesus displayed God's love by becoming
the sacrificial lamb for us on the cross. God chose to send His son, Jesus,
to be the atoning sacrifice for our sins. Could you imagine sending your
own child to make a similar sacrifice? Can you imagine a loving father
sending his son to be crucified on a cross? That's exactly what God, the
father, did for you. He sent Jesus, His son, to die on the cross as a perfect
sacrifice for the atonement of your sins. God chose this to be the option
available for a fallen mankind to be able to come into a relationship with
Him. We can be assured Jesus represents the very essence of love because
He reflects the Father's nature. I feel blessed knowing the authority to
open the seals resides with Jesus. I know we can rely on a God whose very
essence is love to obtain the answers we need to fulfill the unique purpose

He blesses us with in serving in His kingdom. Authority to open the seals resides with Jesus. We can be confident in going to Him for answers we need. In fact, I would argue we should seek those answers only from Him through reading His holy word, diligent prayer, and listening for the prompts provided to us from the Holy Spirit. We should listen to what the Holy Spirit says to us as we pray for answers, we need to follow the purpose God has blessed us with in His kingdom.

TRUMPETS AND BOWLS

WE SHOULD EXPECT JESUS TO correct and refine us through trials and tribulation. We can look at the judgments in Revelations to reveal how He might reveal himself to a fallen and wicked world, a world that never accepted Him as their savior. We should look at these examples through the lens of the judgments being handed out by a loving God. God seeks only to correct us, so we may repent and turn to Him. This is the posture Christians should take when walking through times of correction, rebuke, and tribulation in their lives. We should try to figure out what God's trying to communicate to us. In looking at these judgments being handed out by God in the book of Revelation we must also understand God's imposing these judgments on populations that don't know and don't recognize Him. As a result, His judgments may seem extremely severe. We must understand this may be necessary to gain the attention of these populations. The trumpet judgments can be found in Revelation chapters 8 and 9.

The following provides a summarization of the trumpet judgments:

TRUMPET JUDGMENT:	NOTES CONCERNING THE JUDGMENT:
The first trumpet: (Revelation 8:7) "Hail and fire mixed with blood," One third of the world's trees are burned up in this judgment, and all the grass is consumed.	Natural disasters including great hailstorms and wildfires will consume a third of the trees and all the grasslands.
The second trumpet: (Revelation 8:8). The result is something like a huge mountain, all ablaze, being thrown into the sea (perhaps a meteor strike).	A third of the sea turns to blood. A third of the ships are destroyed, and a third of all ocean life dies. Notice here God smites the salt water (oceans) before smiting fresh water (required for drinking by mankind).

The third trumpet: (Revelation 8:10). The third trumpet is like the second trumpet, except this plague affects the world's freshwater lakes and rivers instead of the oceans. Specifically, "A great star, blazing like a torch", falls from the sky and poisons a third of the fresh water supply.	God smites the fresh water required for mankind to drink. The star is given the name "Wormwood" because wormwood is a plant with a bitter flavor. The star "Wormwood" will make much of the drinking water bitter. Many will die because of a lack of an adequate supply of drinking water.
The fourth trumpet: (Revelation 8:12). This trumpet brings about changes in the heavens. A third of the sun was struck, a third of the moon, and a third of the stars, so that a third of them turned dark. A third of the day was without light, and a third of the night was without the moon's light.	This judgment affects celestial bodies. Following the blowing of the 4th trumpet a special warning is provided. Revelation 8:13 says, "I saw, and I heard an eagle, flying in mid heaven, saying with a loud voice, "Woe! Woe! Woe for those who dwell on the earth, because of the other voices of the trumpets of the three angels, who are yet to sound!"" Signs within the celestial bodies may be warnings to mankind that demons are being provided more authority to harm them.
Fifth trumpet: Locusts/demons are released to torment the wicked people on the earth for a limited amount of time (five months).	The fifth, sixth, and seventh trumpets are referred to as the three woes. The wicked are stung for five months by locusts/demons. There is a clear distinction here between righteous and wicked. The righteous are not affected by this judgment. Again, God's intent is to send a message to the lost so they may repent and return to Him.
Sixth trumpet: Four bound demons are released to kill a third of humanity with an army.	God unleashes demons to kill a third of humanity.

The Seventh trumpet: Ushers in the last and final series of judgments – the bowl judgments.

God provides an interlude here. He pauses between the time of the sixth and seventh trumpet. The seventh trumpet provides a prophecy of Jesus' second coming and the final judgment of mankind. Prior to His return, however, there will be the next series of plagues represented as the bowl judgments. They are much harsher than the trumpet judgments. After the blowing of the sixth trumpet the angels are provided with bowls to be poured out on humanity. The seven bowl judgments then take place.

THE BOWL JUDGMENTS AND THE TWO WITNESS:

After the trumpets have sounded, they are followed by "seven bowls of wrath poured out upon the earth." These bowls are described in Revelation chapter 16. God also provides two holy witnesses (in Revelation 11) to the remaining remnant of His believers at some point during the bowl judgments. The two holy witnesses will be provided during the tribulation period. We know this to be true because at the beginning of the verse introducing the two holy witnesses John is asked to measure the temple. As a result, it is clear the temple must exist at the time when the two holy witnesses appear.

The following is a summary of the bowl judgments.

BOWL JUDGMENT:	NOTES CONCERNING THE JUDGMENT:
First Bowl Judgment: Those who bore the Mark of the beast and worshiped the image suffered painful sores.	Those following God are completely immune to the effects of the first bowl judgment, but those following the beast are not immune. Here God makes a distinction between the wicked and righteous.
Second Bowl Judgment: Seas of blood.	The sea had already lost a third of the life contained in it with the sounding of the second trumpet (Rev:8-9). Now the rest of life within the oceans is gone.

Third Bowl Judgment: The rivers of blood.	All fresh water on the face of the planet is transformed into blood.

Note the two holy witnesses must appear prior to this point in time. This is because they are said to have the power to turn water into blood. After this point, all the water on the face of the planet (both salt water and fresh water) would have been turned into blood. The two holy witnesses are said to provide their testimony for three-and-a-half years. As a result, I believe this will be during the second half of the tribulation period.

Fourth Bowl Judgment: The scorching sun.	More signs in the heavens from celestial bodies. God permits the sun to scorch the earth's inhabitants.
Fifth Bowl Judgment: Darkness. Here God causes the throne of the beast to be covered in darkness.	This will be an unusual darkness like what happened in Egypt during the times of the Egyptian plagues. The darkness will only affect the beast's Kingdome. Again, a distinction is made by God between the kingdom of the beast and other righteous believers.
Sixth Bowl Judgment: War. The great river Euphrates is dried up. This prepares the way for the beast and false prophet to move against the remaining faithful in God.	The great river Euphrates is dried up opening a path for the kings of the East to attack God's elect. This may also be representative of the killing of the two holy witnesses
Seventh Bowl Judgment: God's fury.	Signs will take place in the heavens. A super earthquake will take place, an earthquake of a magnitude never seen previously. Jesus' second coming will take place. The final judgment will be poured out by God on all of humanity. Note the great earthquake may provide protection for God's remnant of believers. Jerusalem will be split into three parts. Splitting Jerusalem in this manner will likely disrupt the beast's army from being able to wage war against the remaining remnant of God's believers. This will be viewed as a miraculous saving of His people.

If we really examine what's going on in the book of Revelation, a clear picture is painted of a God who is handing out these plagues in a very specific order to gain the attention of the population of earth. Note the progression of plagues is outlined within the pages of the Bible. God is not handing out these plagues as a matter of pure rage against humanity. No, He is handing out the plagues in the very progression they are outlined within the pages of the Bible. He is sending a clear message to humanity to repent and return to Him. God wants humanity to turn to Him so they might be saved. These judgments are extremely harsh but notice several things about how the judgments are being handed out by God.

- The plagues grow progressively worse As an example, God smites salt water before He smites fresh water. This is proof there is a specific progression to His judgments on mankind.
- The trumpets are handed to the angels first. This is God's attempt to send us a warning prior to imposing the harsher bowl judgments.
- The bowls are ushered in only after the completion of six of the seven trumpet judgments. There is even a pause before proceeding to the bowl judgments. Again, this provides evidence God is following a very specific progression where the judgments get progressively more and more severe.
- The first bowl judgment draws a clear distinction between the righteous and wicked. This is a merciful act by a loving God and serves as a sign to the population of the earth there is a distinction between the wicked and the righteous.
- The judgments get progressively worse as God tries to draw an unrepentant humanity back to Him, but they progress in a manner that has already been foretold by God within the pages of the Bible. The intent of the judgments is to serve as a warning to mankind in a desire to have them repent and turn to Him.
- God finally takes away the two holy witnesses He sent to earth to proclaim His message of repentance to mankind. At this point, there is no longer any active spiritual message left on the face of the planet beyond the last remnant of believers remaining on the earth at this time. This is not the end of the story, however, because even at this point (this late in God's judgments) God gives three-and-a-half more days before His return. This may represent the sign of Jesus being in the tomb and Jonah being in the belly of the great fish for three days. These three-and-a-half days

provide one last opportunity for mankind to repent and turn to God. The wine press (judgment carried out by the angels against mankind) is only initiated after the three-and-a-half days have expired and the two holy witnesses are resurrected and brought up to be with God upon Jesus' second coming.

Some may question how a loving God could impose such horrific judgments and plagues upon His creation. We must understand the judgments and plagues God is handing out to humanity during this time is being handed out to people that have utterly walked away from Him. These judgments must be severe to gain the attention of the people He is seeking to call to Him. Many of the people that are having these judgments poured out upon them have either never accepted Him or have openly rejected Him as their savior. Some may have never read the Bible. As a result, it's necessary to send harsh judgments on this population to gain their attention. I would also say we must have faith in God's perfect justice. We must simply have faith God will act in a perfectly justifiable manner. We must recognize, as Christians, we have been provided the responsibility to spread the gospel to all people. This is known as the Great Commission.

> But the eleven disciples went into Galilee, to the mountain where Jesus had sent them. When they saw him, they bowed down to him; but some doubted. Jesus came to them and spoke to them, saying, "All authority has been given to me in heaven and on earth. Go and make disciples of all nations, baptizing them in the name of the Father and of the Son and of the Holy Spirit, teaching them to observe all things that I commanded you. Behold, I am with you always, even to the end of the age. Matthew 28:16-20

Jesus provided the Great Commission to all His followers. We are to carry the good news of the gospel to all nations of the world. We are to make disciples of all nations so they will have heard the good news of the gospel. My prayer is that we, as Christians, are diligent in carrying out the Great Commission so that perhaps people from all nations may have read their Bibles and may not suffer through these plagues. It's important to remember the following:

- The Bible tells us how we are to recognize the nature of the antichrist. It tells us anyone that does not acknowledge Jesus' birth, death, and resurrection has the spirit of the antichrist in them. 1 John 2: 22-23 says, "Who is the liar but he who denies that Jesus is the Christ? This is the Antichrist, he who denies the Father and the Son. Whoever denies the Son doesn't have the Father. He who confesses the Son has the Father also."

- We can have assurance God is love. He is the very essence of love. Jesus is the perfect reflection of God's character. As a result, when God rebukes us, we can have confidence He rebukes you as a father rebukes his son (in love). He will do anything within His power not to lose you. The picture painted here is of a God whose very essence is love.

- God allows free choice. He allows free choice in everything He's created. Angels, Satan, demons, mankind, nations, kingdoms, and influential leaders all have free choice. God is sovereign over all of them. This is His story, but He gives us the blessing of free choice to make our own decisions. We are to participate in His story by walking on a path outlined by the Godly purpose He lays out for us.

- You are provided with a unique purpose in His story. You can find your purpose by earnestly seeking Him through prayer and searching the word of God. Listen for how the Holy Spirit might be answering your prayers and prompting you to act.

- God's provision of His word in advance to communicate the signs and judgments He will use to draw humanity back to Him shows He is a God of mercy and love. He's not simply punishing mankind to punish them. He is bringing judgments upon them in a very specific order of progression to send them a clear message of repentance. He decided at the very beginning of His creation the progression of these judgments. He communicated them in incredible detail within the pages of the Bible. It is His desire to bring the lost souls back to Him. He wants you to accept Him and return to His loving embrace.

My sheep hear my voice, and I know them, and they follow me. I give eternal life to them. They will never perish, and no one will snatch them out of my hand. My Father who has given them to me is greater than all. No one is able to snatch them out of my Father's hand." ~ **John 10:27-29**

Going through trials can be difficult. Understand God tests us to refine us. His desire is we would shine as bright as refined gold in His presence. Understanding this fact can help us endure times of tribulation in our own lives. We can see in the book of Revelation examples of how God chose to test an unrepentant and rebellious population. God makes it clear He makes a distinction between the righteous and the wicked. He will be as merciful and gentle as possible to the population of His believers living on the earth at the time these plagues are being unleashed on humanity. This is the picture I want to paint for you in this book. Understand the plagues for what they are. They are God's attempt to draw an unbelieving and unrepentant population toward Him.

Knowing God is love allowed me to re-read the book of Revelation. I have a better understanding that these plagues will contain a distinction between His believers and the wicked and unrepentant population. God will be as loving as possible toward me during this timeframe. Any suffering God allows me to go through during these plagues will be done to simply help refine me so I may be as pure as gold in His loving presence. If you are one of His followers, be assured God works everything toward your ultimate good. You must trust God when going through trials and tribulations. He will be as merciful as possible on His followers during times of tribulation and trial. These times certainly won't be easy for His followers, but God has never promised us an easy path through life. God promises, however, that once we have accepted Him as our savior, He will guide us, nurture us, and protect us. Such is the promise made to His believers during the time of the Great Tribulation.

THE MODERN REBIRTH OF ISRAEL

ISRAEL WAS CONQUERED IN 135 AD by Rome. There was no nation of Israel between 135AD and 1947 and yet, Israel was able to re-emerge as a sovereign nation in 1947. This was truly a miraculous event, and there are prophetic Bible verses that speak to Israel re-emerging as a sovereign nation in these modern times. Again, this speaks to God's sovereignty over the nations. There are a few prophetic Bible verses that speak to Israel re-emerging as a sovereign nation.

> They will fly down on the shoulders of the Philistines on the west. Together they will plunder the children of the east. They will extend their power over Edom and Moab, and the children of Ammon will obey them. ~ **Isaiah 11:14**

The above Bible verse speaks to the events that took place in Israel's War of Independence of 1948-49, and the subsequent six-day war fought in 1967. In those wars Israel fought with the Palestinians. It should be noted the location of Palestine, called Philistia existed over 2,500 years ago. Philistia existed in the southwestern portion of the region now known as Palestine. This represents the slopes of Philistia that is called out in the above Bible verse. During Israel's 1948-49 War of Independence, Palestinians were scattered throughout the surrounding Arab states as described in the above Bible verse as the Jewish nation of Israel flew down on them causing them to scatter to escape to the relative safety of the surrounding Arab world. One home for the Palestinian refugees became the Gaza strip. (This exactly corresponds to the territory associated with ancient Philistia.) Israel then moved toward the Gaza strip in the early hours of the six-day war. Jewish troops, tanks, and planes again flew down on these Philistinians (Palestinians) to the West, conquering the territory as Isaiah foretold in the verses above.

In this same prophecy Isaiah tells us the future reborn Israel will "Plunder the children of the east." They will "extend their power over Edom and Moab." The prophecy also says the "Ammonites will be subject to them." In the Six-Day war, the Egyptian territories of Gaza and Sinai were conquered. Israel also attacked eastward in both the Jordanian-annexed West Bank region as well as the strategic highlands of Golan on their northern front with Syria. These territories were quickly conquered and continue to be held by Israel today. Thus, the newly formed sovereign nation of Israel truly did plunder the nations to the east as Isaiah predicted in the above Bible verse. Israel's most prized possession from the six-day war came when Jewish forces took hold of the ancient city of Jerusalem against the defending army of Jordan. As a result of the six-day war, many Arab people became displaced from the West Bank and Gaza areas – hundreds of thousands of them fled the ravages of war into the surrounding Arab nations. The Bible speaks of this as well, in the third chapter of the book of Joel. The Bible verses provide prophetic accounts of the activities of a regathered Israel. They predicted Israel would bring ravage upon their ancient enemies. The enemies in this case would be the descendants of the people who originally participated in scattering the Jews from their land in addition to those who gloated over their plight.

> . . . and have cast lots for my people, and have given a boy for a prostitute, and sold a girl for wine, that they may drink. "Yes, and what are you to me, Tyre, and Sidon, and all the regions of Philistia? Will you repay me? And if you repay me, I will swiftly and speedily return your repayment on your own head. Because you have taken my silver and my gold, and have carried my finest treasures into your temples, and have sold the children of Judah and the children of Jerusalem to the sons of the Greeks, that you may remove them far from their border. Behold, I will stir them up out of the place where you have sold them and will return your repayment on your own head; and I will sell your sons and your daughters into the hands of the children of Judah, and they will sell them to the men of Sheba, to a faraway nation, for Yahweh has spoken it. ~ **Joel 3:3-8**

The first part of these Bible verses describes numerous evils done to the Jews during the times of their scattering. Even though Israel remained under God's judgment, the Lord never condoned the actions taken by those nations used to punish Israel. Israel's displacement of the Palestinians was foretold in the Bible as an event that would take place by the re-gathered nation of Israel, precisely as it took place when Israel was again permitted to become a sovereign nation. Today, nearly 1.5 million Palestinians, or about one third of them, live in 58 identified refugee camps within Lebanon, Syria, Jordan, the Gaza strip, and the West Bank areas. They have been scatted as described in the above Bible verse. The remaining two thirds have been scattered into the entire Arab world – precisely as Joel prophesized in the above Bible verses. Many displaced Palestinians live under Israeli control within Gaza and the West Bank areas to this day. It is clear to see the regathered nation of Israel displaced and ravaged many of their ancient enemies, precisely as Joel predicted.

One cannot understate the importance of Israel re-emerging as a sovereign nation with respect to what it means for Bible end time prophecy. In the end times the antichrist is said to sign a treaty with the nation of Israel for seven years that will permit Israel to re-build the temple of their God and resume sacrifices at the temple for the first three-and-a-half years of that treaty. Prior to Israel becoming a sovereign nation there would have been no nation to negotiate a treaty with, so we can see, once again, God is in control and the events that are happening today all align with the prophetic accounts that must take place within the Bible that led up to these final days.

WAR IN THE MIDDLE EAST

CURRENT EVENTS BETWEEN ISRAEL, SYRIA, and Iran raise concerns of a potential war in the Middle East. Some prophetic Bible verses appear to describe the nature of a future war in the Middle East. We will examine these prophetic Bible verses to gain a better understand of what a future war in the middle east might encompass as it relates to the nation of Israel. Psalm 83 represents a prayer from the prophet Asaph. Asaph, being recognized as a prophet, leads many to conclude the prayer resulted from a vision of a future war. There is no historic evidence of Israel ever fighting against the exact conglomeration of nations contained within these Bible verses in a single war. Consequently, many believe Psalm 83 may be speaking of a future war between Israel and this conglomeration of nations:

> God, don't keep silent. Don't keep silent, and don't be still, God. For, behold, your enemies are stirred up. Those who hate you have lifted up their heads. They conspire with cunning against your people. They plot against your cherished ones. "Come," they say, "let's destroy them as a nation, that the name of Israel may be remembered no more." For they have conspired together with one mind. They form an alliance against you. The tents of Edom and the Ishmaelites; Moab, and the Hagrites; Gebal, Ammon, and Amalek; Philistia with the inhabitants of Tyre; Assyria also is joined with them. They have helped the children of Lot. Selah. Do to them as you did to Midian, as to Sisera, as to Jabin, at the river Kishon; who perished at Endor, who became as dung for the earth. Make their nobles like Oreb and Zeeb, yes, all their princes like Zebah and Zalmunna, who said, "Let's take possession of God's pasture lands." My God, make them like tumbleweed, like chaff before the wind. As the fire that burns the forest, as the flame that sets the mountains on fire, so pursue them with your tempest, and terrify them with your storm. Fill their faces with confusion, that they may seek your name, Yahweh. Let them be disappointed and dismayed forever. Yes, let them be confounded and perish; that they may know that you alone, whose name is Yahweh, are the Most High over all the earth. -**Psalm 83**

THE NATIONS INVOLVED IN THE PSALMS 83 WAR INCLUDE THE FOLLOWING:

ANCIENT BIBLICAL POPULATION:	CURRENT NATION:
Edom, Moab, Gebal & Ammon	Jordan
Ishmaelites and Hagrites	Saudi Arabia
Amalek	Egypt
Philistia	Gaza and Palestine
Tyre	Lebanon
Assyria	Syria and Iraq
Children of Lot	Scattered throughout the Middle East

The purpose of the war will be to completely destroy Israel. Some believe the Psalm 83 war took place as part of the 6-Day war.[11] They believe this because the nations of Egypt, Syria, and Jordan aligned against Israel with the stated objective to completely destroy Israel. As a result, some portion of Psalm 83 may have been a prophetic account of the 6-Day war. There are some details, however, which simply don't exactly align with the 6-Day war. First, there are several identified nations within Psalm 83 that did not take part in the 6-Day war. Those nations include Saudi Arabia, Iraq, and Lebanon. Also, many would argue the result of the Psalm 83 war should be the complete destruction of all the nations that took part in the war against Israel. Since Egypt, Jordan, and Syria still exist, many say the 6-Day war is not a good candidate for the Psalm 83 war. I am not sure if Psalm 83 represented the 6-Day war or if these Bible verses speak to a future war. I could be persuaded in either direction but there are other Bible verses that are prophetic in speaking about a future war in the Middle East. These Bible verses speak to the nations of

---

[11]   Gary, "Psalm 83: The Six-Day War", Unsealed, July 19, 2017, *https://www. unsealed.org/2017/07/psalm-83-six-day-war.html*

Syria and Iran, two nations currently at enmity with Israel.

> Yahweh of Armies says: 'Behold, I will break the bow of Elam, the chief of their might. I will bring on Elam the four winds from the four quarters of the sky and will scatter them toward all those winds. There will be no nation where the outcasts of Elam will not come. I will cause Elam to be dismayed before their enemies, and before those who seek their life. I will bring evil on them, even my fierce anger,' says Yahweh; 'and I will send the sword after them, until I have consumed them. ~ **Jeremiah 49:35-37**

Here are some key things to consider as we read the above verses from Jeremiah:

- Modern day Iran is currently composed of ancient Elam and Persia.
- Jeremiah predicts a portion of Iran (Elam's portion) will suffer the fate of a broken bow. Additionally, he declares Elam will be struck at the mainstay of their might, which today could refer to an attack upon Iran's nuclear program that currently resides in ancient Elam.
- One of Iran's most strategic and vulnerable nuclear targets is the Bushehr nuclear reactor, located in the heart of ancient Elam.[12]
- The destruction of this nuclear reactor would cause the inhabitants to seek refuge in other countries. The ecological catastrophe (like Chernobyl) would require the inhabitants to seek refuge in other areas of the Middle East, as is precisely described in the above Bible verse.
- It's interesting that this prophetic Bible verse doesn't speak of a curse against Persia. As stated above, Iran is currently made up of two ancient Biblical populations (Persia and Elam). This may be evidence that this curse may represent a strategic strike against Iran that targets only Elam's portion of Iran.

Modern day Iran is working closely with the nation of Syria. They have been working together to manufacture military equipment. Israeli Defense Minister Benny Gantz said Iran is using more than ten military

---

[12]   Dr. David R. Reagan, "The Prophecy of Elam", Lamb and Lion Ministries, _https://christinprophecy.org/articles/the-prophecy-of-elam/_

facilities in Syria to produce advanced missiles and weapons for its prox-ies.[13] Attacks have been made by Israel during the past several years on what is described as Iranian-linked targets in Syria. Iran is producing mid and long-range missiles, along with other weapons, from these sites in Syria. If Israel believes Iran is working with Syria to build missiles, Israel will likely continue to strike these sites of production in Syria and Iran as they have done in the past.

Finally, consider two passages, one from Isaiah 17 (the whole chap-ter) and one from Jeremiah 49: 23-27. Taken together they say Damascus will be destroyed. Damascus boasts of having the oldest constantly popu-lated city on the face of the planet, and it is likely to be destroyed as fore-told in these prophetic Bible verses.[14] In addition, these Bible passages provide indication Israel will be severely shaken as a nation. We will look at specific Bible verses from Isaiah and Jeremiah that may be speaking about a future war between Israel and Syria.

SECTION OF BIBLE VERSE:	POTENTIAL MEANING:
Isaiah 17:1 "Behold, Damascus is taken away from being a city, and it will be a ruinous heap"	Damascus will be destroyed. The city will become a heap of ruins.
Isaiah 17:2 "The cities of Aroer are forsak-en. They will be for flocks, which shall lie down, and no one shall make them afraid."	The cities of Syria will be deserted forever. They will become a pasture for sheep and cattle, and no one will drive them away.

---

13   Reuters, "Israeli minister says Iran using Syria facilities for weapons production", Reuters, September 22, 2022, _https://www.reuters.com/world/middle-east/ israeli-minister-says-iran-using-syria-facilities-weapons-production-2022-09- 12/#:~:text=JERUSALEM%2C%20Sept%2012%20_%28Reuters%29%20-%20 Israeli%20Defence%20Minister,it%20has%20described%20as%20Iranian-linked%20targets%20in%20Syria.

14   Britt Gillette "The Coming Destruction of Damascus", End Times Bible Prophecy Understanding God's Prophetic Word, http://www.end-times-bible-prophecy.com/ the-coming-destruction-of-damascus.html#:~:text=The%20prophet%20Isaiah%20 says%20Damascus%20will%20disappear%2C%20become,Damascus%20 and%20killed%20its%20king%20%282%20Kings%2016%3A9%29.

Isaiah 17:4-5 "It will happen in that day that the glory of Jacob will be made thin, and the fatness of his flesh will become lean. It will be like when the harvester gathers the wheat, and his arm reaps the grain. Yes, it will be like when one gleans grain in the valley of Rephaim."	This portion of the prophetic verses speak directly to Israel being severely shaken and becoming much weaker as a nation because of this war.
Isaiah 17:6 "Yet gleanings will be left there, like the shaking of an olive tree, two or three olives in the top of the uppermost bough, four or five in the outermost branches of a fruitful tree, says Yahweh, the God of Israel."	This verse makes it clear Israel won't be completely destroyed. God will allow Israel to be weakened by other nations, but He won't allow Israel to be snuffed out of existence completely. This also speaks to those left in Israel. They will reside upon fruitful boughs, meaning their hearts will be pre-disposed to turn toward their God after this war.
Isaiah 17:7-8 "In that day, people will look to their Maker, and their eyes will have respect for the Holy One of Israel. They will not look to the altars, the work of their hands; neither shall they respect that which their fingers have made, either the Asherah poles, or the incense altars.	When the days come when Israel is permitted to be severely shaken by this war the remnant that remain in Israel will turn for help from their creator, the Holy God of Israel. They will no longer rely upon the altars they made with their own hands, or trust in their own handiwork.
Isaiah 17:9 "In that day, their strong cities will be like the forsaken places in the woods and on the mountain top, which were forsaken from before the children of Israel; and it will be a desolation."	When this day comes, well-defended cities will be deserted and left in ruins.
Isaiah 17:10-11 "For you have forgotten the God of your salvation, and have not remembered the rock of your strength. Therefore you plant pleasant plants, and set out foreign seedlings. In the day of your planting, you hedge it in. In the morning, you make your seed blossom, but the harvest flees away in the day of grief and of desperate sorrow."	This verse is communicating the reason that God allowed Israel to be so severely shaken. God is communicating that Israel has forgotten the God who rescues and protects them like a mighty rock. It is stating that although they planted sacred gardens to worship foreign gods, they have come to nothing (there would be no harvest from that worship of other foreign gods).

Isaiah 17:12-14 "Ah, the uproar of many peoples, who roar like the roaring of the seas; and the rushing of nations, that rush like the rushing of mighty waters! The nations will rush like the rushing of many waters: but he will rebuke them, and they will flee far off, and will be chased like the chaff of the mountains before the wind, and like the whirling dust before the storm. At evening, behold, terror! Before the morning, they are no more. This is the portion of those who plunder us, and the lot of those who rob us."

This Bible verse states that God will reprimand the many nations that rage against Him. This Bible verse is also stating those nations will retreat from Israel, driven away like dust. This set of Bible verses may be a prophetic utterance to the Gog/Magog war (spoken about in the next chapter of this book) as it states, "At evening, behold, terror! Before morning, they are no more. This is the portion of those who plunder us, and the lot of those who rob us."

The Bible provides prophetic verses that speak to future wars in the Middle East. As a result of future wars in the Middle East God might permit Israel to be severely shaken as a nation. The surviving remnant of Israel, however, will give thanks to God. They will rely upon Him for their protection. Their hearts will be fully turned back toward their God after this war. As a result of the war Israel will lose a lot of their strength, but God will cause many to re-gather in Israel from other nations of the world. Israel will eventually recover from war and will again become wealthy as a nation. Israel will likely give up a great deal of their military strength as their hearts will be fully turned toward their God for their protection. This may have the appearance to other surrounding nations that they no longer have a hedge of protection. This misconception might usher in the Gog/Magog war.

THE GOG/MAGOG WAR

THE BIBLE PROVIDES PROPHETIC VERSES about another future war against Israel in which many nations will unite against her. The purpose and outcome of the war are different from the previous prophetic Bible verses. The purpose of the Gog/Magog war will be to take plunder from Israel, not to completely destroy her as a nation. The outcome of the Gog/Magog war will be that God alone will save Israel in miraculous manner. Chapters 38 and 39 of Ezekiel describe this future war against Israel.

THE NATIONS INVOLVED IN THE GOG/MAGOG WAR INCLUDE:[15]

ANCIENT BIBLICAL POPULATION:	CURRENT NATION:
Gog	Russia
Magog	Central Asia
Meshech	Turkey
Tubal	Turkey
Persia (note that Elam is not mentioned here)	Iran
Ethiopia	Sudan
Put	Libya
Gomer	Turkey
Togarmah	Turkey

---

[15] Dillon Burroughs, "Who are Gog, Magog, Tarshish, and other nations of Ezekiel 38?", Blogos, May 14, 2013, https://www.blogos.org/exploringtheword/Gog-Magog-Tarshish.php

A special note should be mentioned here. As we noted in the previous chapter of this book there are two ancient populations that make up the nation of Iran. Those nations include Persia and Elam. As you can see here, Elam is not mentioned as being a nation that will take part in the Gog/Magog war. I believe the answer to this is simple. Elam would have been destroyed via the prophecy spoken about in the previous chapter of this book. As a result, that ancient population of Iran won't be able to take part in the Gog and Magog war against Israel.

SELECTIONS FROM EZEKIEL'S PROPHECY (CHAPTERS 38 AND 39):

SECTION OF BIBLE VERSE:	BIBLE VERSE MEANING:
Ezekiel 39:12 "The house of Israel will be burying them for seven months, that they may cleanse the land."	Israel will spend seven months burying the dead from this war. The number seven represents completeness in the Bible. This Bible verse may not refer to an exact seven-month period but may mean the number of months necessary to complete the task of burying bodies to cleanse the land.
Ezekiel 39:9 "Those who dwell in the cities of Israel will go out, and will make fires of the weapons and burn them, both the shields and the bucklers, the bows and the arrows, and the war clubs and the spears, and they will make fires with them for seven years;"	The weapons of the armies of Gog and Magog are to be burned as fuel for seven years. Russia and China are nuclear powers, so perhaps this means Israel might use nuclear materials for seven years to make energy for themselves after the conclusion of this war. Also note the seven years spoken of in this Biblical prophecy might align with the fact that this war might take place just prior to the start of the tribulation period. If this is the case Israel wouldn't need to burn weapons for fuel after seven years because Jesus would have returned at the end of the seven-year tribulation period.

Ezekiel 38:8-12 "After many days you will be visited. In the latter years you will come into the land that is brought back from the sword, that is gathered out of many peoples, on the mountains of Israel, which have been a continual waste; but it is brought out of the peoples, and they will dwell securely, all of them. You will ascend. You will come like a storm. You will be like a cloud to cover the land, you, and all your hordes, and many peoples with you." The Lord Yahweh says: "It will happen in that day that things will come into your mind, and you will devise an evil plan. You will say, I will go up to the land of unwalled villages. I will go to those who are at rest, who dwell securely, all of them dwelling without walls, and having neither bars nor gates, to take the plunder and to take prey; to turn your hand against the waste places that are inhabited, and against the people who are gathered out of the nations, who have gotten livestock and goods, who dwell in the middle of the earth.'"

When this prophecy speaks about a country "dwelling without walls and having neither bars nor gates." This refers to a country lacking a noticeable hedge of protection. This may refer to Israel after they have recovered from the war discussed in the previous chapter of this book. Israel will come out of that war severely shaken, but their hearts will be turned back toward their God such that they may not rebuild a massive military for their protection. They will, instead, rely upon God for their protection. This prophecy is saying Gog and Magog will seek to move against Israel. They will perceive Israel's lack of a hedge of protection as weakness. Israel will appear to be easy prey for plunder for those nations that chose to move against her.

It should also be noted here that this prophetic Bible verse clearly states that Israel will be in a state of recovering from a previous war when the Gog and Magog war takes place. As a result, we have verification that there will be at least one war in Israel prior to the outbreak of the Gog and Magog war (as described within this book).

Ezekiel 38: 19-22 "For in my jealousy and in the fire of my wrath I have spoken. Surely in that day there will be a great shaking in the land of Israel; so that the fish of the sea, the birds of the sky, the animals of the field, all creeping things who creep on the earth, and all the men who are on the surface of the earth will shake at my presence. Then the mountains will be thrown down, the steep places will fall, and every wall will fall to the ground. I will call for a sword against him to all my mountains," says the Lord Yahweh. "Every man's sword will be against his brother.

This portion of the prophecy signifies God will fight directly on Israel's behalf. He will explode in furious wrath against the invading armies of Gog and Magog. They will be destroyed by His wrath in a supernatural manner.

I will enter into judgment with him with pestilence and with blood. I will rain on him, and on his hordes, and on the many peoples who are with him, an overflowing shower, with great hailstones, fire, and sulfur."

Ezekiel 38:23 "I will magnify myself, and sanctify myself, and I will make myself known in the eyes of many nations. Then they will know that I am Yahweh."	The victory will be unmistakably provided at the hands of the Lord and God will be glorified as a direct result of the war.

Or consider these verses from Zechariah:

This is the plague with which the Lord will strike all the nations that fought against Jerusalem: Their flesh will rot while they are still standing on their feet, their eyes will rot in their sockets, and their tongues will rot in their mouths. On that day people will be stricken by the Lord with great panic. They will seize each other by the hand and attack one another. Judah too will fight at Jerusalem. The wealth of all the surrounding nations will be collected—great quantities of gold and silver and clothing. A similar plague will strike the horses and mules, the camels and donkeys, and all the animals in those camps. Then the survivors from all the nations that have attacked Jerusalem will go up year after year to worship the King, the Lord Almighty, and to celebrate the Festival of Tabernacles. ~ **Zechariah 14: 12-16 NIV**

There are a few things of note to be taken from the above prophetic Bible verses:

- This plague will be from the hand of the Lord.
- The plague will be limited to the nations invading Israel.
- The plague will come swiftly. People will still be standing on their feet when they begin to rot.
- Glory will be given to God for bringing His plague against these nations.
- God will be praised for making a swift and just judgment.
- There will be great panic and confusion within the nations under God's plague.

Shortly after the Gog/Magog war I believe a treaty will be signed that allows Israel to rebuild God's temple. A portion of the surviving remnant of the war will repent and turn to the Lord as their God. They will have witnessed a miraculous event in both the war and the subsequent plague at the hands of God. God will use this as a tool to get the attention of many living in the invading nations to repent and turn to Him. The Bible says the remnant populations from those nations will take part in the Festival of Tabernacles. It's important to point out only people converted to Judaism can take part in this festival. This reflects a softening of hearts toward Israel after this war.

God tells us in advance what will happen in the Gog/Magog war so He can show us how He will deal with these nations. Ultimately God's intent is to bring glory to Himself. The one thing I take from this future war and terrible plague is God permits the war to happen so He can show His glory to all nations on earth. Especially to those nations participating in the war. He does this so He can draw the populations of those nations toward Him. There are nations in the world today who might not have another opportunity to see God as their savior. This war will be used as an opportunity by a loving God to gain the attention of these invading nations. We know God is the very essence of love. God can use something as terrible as war and plague for our ultimate good. Everyone on the face of the planet is going to be terrified when this war and subsequent plague takes place. It is certain God will have the attention of everyone on earth when these events take place. I have faith we serve a God who is love. I can feel confident knowing the ultimate good will come from this war and subsequent plague for those who believe in Him. God is in control of everything. What He permits to happen is done with ultimate good in mind for His believers.

THE RISE OF THE MAHDI

CHRISTIANS ARE AWAITING THE SECOND coming of Jesus to judge the world, Jews are eagerly awaiting their Messiah, and Islam is waiting for the emergence of their own savior known as the Mahdi. To gain a better understanding of how the end times might proceed we need to obtain a better understanding of who this mysterious figure is said to be, and the specific signs that Islam is waiting for that will signal the emergence of the Mahdi. In Islam the very meaning of the term Mahdi is said to mean "The guided one".[16] In Islam it is believed the Mahdi will appear shortly before the second coming of Jesus (the Islamic Jesus, not the Christian Jesus – we will discuss this in a subsequent chapter of this book). Together, the Mahdi and Jesus (the Islamic Jesus) will fight against the Dajjal (This is a figure that is identified as an Islamic sort of antichrist.). The Mahdi will be recognized by a lot of signs, many of which include the following:[17]

- The Mahdi will be a direct descendant of the prophet Mohammad through his daughter Fatima.
- The true Mahdi will rise to power in a supernatural manner in a single night.
- All Islamic righteous leaders will agree upon his piety, leadership, and authority in a single night.
- There will be an unmistakable miraculous event that will signal to all Islamic believers worldwide that the true Mahdi has arrived.
- A key sign of the true Mahdi is his sincerity, humility, and fear of Allah with respect to his authority. He does not want to be the Caliph, even though he is righteous, which is exactly what makes him qualified to lead. The Sunnah is to avoid taking leadership positions unless absolutely necessary. Note there is a specific Islamic tradition that states the following: "O Abdur Rahman, do not ask for authority. If it is given to you at your request, you will

---

[16] "Al-Mahdi, the promised Caliph to lead the Ummah", Faith in Allah – There is no God but Allah and Muhammad is His Messenger, *http://www.abuaminaelias.com/al-mahdi-promised-caliph/*

[17] "Al-Mahdi, the promised Caliph to lead the Ummah", Faith in Allah – There is no God but Allah and Muhammad is His Messenger, *http://www.abuaminaelias.com/al-mahdi-promised-caliph/*

be held fully responsible for it. If it is given to you without your request, you will be helped by Allah in it."

- The Mahdi is described as emanating radiance, "his face like the shining full moon," a metaphor that underscores his divine purity and the light he is expected to bring into a world riddled with darkness and despair.
- The Mahdi will have a 'beautiful mole on his face,' a mark distinguishing him amidst the multitude.
- The Mahdi will have 'kohl-marked eyes,' a traditional embellishment that signifies not only his noble heritage but also the depth and intensity of his gaze.
- He is not excessively tall nor distressingly short, but of medium stature, with a round head, broad chest, clear forehead, joined eyebrows, and on his right cheek is a mole as if it were a grain of musk upon a piece of amber.
- On his back are two moles, one the color of his skin and the other resembling the mole of the Prophet Muhammad
- He will have a mole (like the seal of prophethood) under his left shoulder
- Under both his shoulders a mark like the leaf of a poplar tree.
- His scent will be more fragrant than musk.

It is said the Mahdi will arise to power within Islam during a time of civil conflict following the death of a Muslim leader. It is said that many factions will vie against each other for power, so this will be a time of internal struggle and potential civil war within the Islamic community that sets the stage for the Mahdi's arrival. It is said the Mahdi will be recognized by some people and they will seek to force him to be Caliph against his will (demonstrating his humility and fear of Allah). They will pledge allegiance to him in front of the Ka'bah in Mecca. Following the initial pledge an army will be dispatched from Syria to attack the Mahdi and his followers. That army will be swallowed up in the desert – like the miracle of Moses parting of the Red Sea for the Israelites upon their exodus from Egypt. Upon witnessing this miracle all righteous believers of Syria, Iraq, and all throughout the Muslim world will recognize him as the true Mahdi. They will come from all over the Muslim world to pledge their allegiance to him.18 There is a specific Islamic tradition that states the following, "There will be a conflict with the death of a Caliph and a man among the residents of Medina will go out fleeing to Mecca. Some people will come to pledge allegiance to him, although he is unwilling, and they will pledge allegiance to him between the corner of the Ka'bah and the station of Abraham. An army from Syria will be dispatched for him and they will be swallowed in the desert between Mecca and Medina. When the people see that, the saints of Syria and the strong tribes of Iraq will come to him and pledge allegiance to him between the corner and the station." Another Islamic tradition states, "An army will raid the Ka'bah but when they reach a desert land, all of them will be swallowed by the earth."

The emergence of the Mahdi is known to be the first of the major signs of Islam. This is confirmed by ibn Kathir, the renowned Muslim scholar from the eighth century.19 While there are some variations of belief between the Sunni and Shia' sects of Islam, and while certain quarters of Sunni reject him altogether, general belief in the Mahdi is not a sectarian issue within Islam but is universal among most Muslims. In simplest terms, the Mahdi, who as the foreordained leader "will rise" to launch a great social transformation to restore and adjust all things under divine guidance. He is known as the Islamic Messiah and is said he will embody the aspirations of his followers in the restoration of the purity of the faith which will bring true and uncorrupted guidance to all of mankind, creating a just social order and a world free from oppression in which the Islamic revelation will be the norm for all nations.

Throughout the Islamic world today there is a call for the restoration of the Islamic Caliphate. The Caliph (Khalifa) in Islam may be viewed somewhat as the Pope of the Muslims. The Caliph is viewed as the Vice-regent for Allah on the earth. It is important to understand when Muslims call for the restoration of the Caliphate, it is ultimately the Mahdi they are calling for. The Mahdi is the awaited "final Caliph" of Islam. Muslims everywhere will be obligated to follow the Mahdi. There is a specific Islamic tradition that states, "If you see him, go and give

---

18 "Al-Mahdi, the promised Caliph to lead the Ummah", Faith in Allah – There is no God but Allah and Muhammad is His Messenger, *https://www.abuaminaelias.com/al-mahdi-promised-caliph/*

19 "Chapter Four The Mahdi: Islam's Awaited Messiah", Answering Islam, *https://answering-islam.org/Authors/JR/Future/ch04_the_mahdi.htm*

him your allegiance, even if you have to crawl over ice, because he is the Vice-regent (Khalifa) of Allah, the Mahdi".

It is said the Mahdi will have control over the wind and the rain and the crops. Under the Mahdi's rule, the world will live in prosperity. Islamic tradition relates that Muhammad once said: "In the last days of my Ummah, universal Islamic community, the Mahdi will appear. Allah will give him power over the wind and the rain, and the earth will bring forth its foliage. He will give away wealth profusely, flocks will be in abundance, and the Ummah will be large and honored. In those years my community will enjoy a time of happiness such as they have never experienced before. Heaven will send rain upon them in torrents, the earth will not withhold any of its plants, and wealth will be available to all. A man will stand and say, "Give to me Mahdi!" and he will say, "Take." As a result of the numerous benefits that the Mahdi brings, it is said all the inhabitants of the Earth will be possessed with a deep love of him. Allah will sow love of him in the hearts of all people. The Prophet said (about the Mahdi), "He will divide the property, and will govern the people by the Sunnah of their Prophet and establish Islam on Earth. He will remain seven years, then die, and the Muslims will pray over him. Notice the anticipated seven-year reign of the Mahdi and how it coincides with the seven-year reign of the Christian antichrist.

While there is more than one tradition regarding the nature and timing of the Mahdi's ascendancy to power, there is one Islamic tradition that places this event at the time of a final treaty between the Arabs and the Romans ("Romans" should be interpreted as referring to Christians, or more generally, the West). Although this treaty is made with the "Romans", it is said to be mediated specifically through a Jew from the priestly lineage of Aaron. The treaty will be made for a period of seven years. Rasulullah (Muhammad) said: "There will be four agreements between you and the Romans (Christians). The fourth agreement will be mediated through a person who will be from the progeny of Hadrat Haroon (Honorable Aaron – Moses' brother) and will be upheld for seven years.[20] It appears the period of this seven-year treaty will likewise be the period of the Mahdi's reign. I believe the treaty will be signed and will signal the start of the Mahdi's reign. This same treaty is foretold within the pages

---

[20]   "Chapter Four The Mahdi: Islam's Awaited Messiah", Answering Islam, *https://answering-islam.org/Authors/JR/Future/ch04_the_mahdi.htm*

of the Bible that signals the agreement between Israel and the antichrist, and I believe the reign of the Mahdi within Islam will arrive at about the same time this treaty is signed between Israel and the nations that took part in the Gog/Magog war.

There are other similarities between the Islamic Mahdi and the Christian antichrist, but one of the most striking similarities comes from Islamic tradition that states The Mahdi is believed to ride on a white horse. Quite interestingly, this tradition is based on the Muslim interpretation of Christian Scriptures. Even though Muslims view the Bible as having been changed and corrupted by Jews and Christians, they still claim to believe that some portions of the "original" inspired books are still to be found within the "corrupted" Bible. As such there exists a tradition within Islamic scholarship that seeks to extract those portions of the Bible Muslims feel may be untainted by the corrupting influence of Jews and Christians. These Judeo-Christian traditions are called by Muslims, isra'iliyyat. One such transmitter of biblical traditions is Muslim scholar Ka'b al-Ahbar. He is viewed among Muslims as a trustworthy transmitter of Muslim tradition as well as isra'iliyyat. Ka'b al-Ahbar is supported in his view that this description of the rider on the white horse as found in the Book of Revelation is indeed the Mahdi by two well-known Egyptian authors, Muhammad Ibn 'Izzat and Muhammad 'Arif in their book Al Mahdi and the End of Time. 'Izzat and Arif quote Ka'b al Ahbar as saying, "I find the Mahdi recorded in the books of the Prophets. For instance, the Book of Revelation says: "And I saw and behold a white horse. He that sat on him… went forth conquering and to conquer." 'Izzat and 'Arif then go on to say: It is clear this man is the Mahdi who will ride the white horse and judge by the Qur'an (with justice) and with whom will be men with marks of prostration on their foreheads, Marks on their foreheads from bowing in prayer with their head to the ground five times daily. It is said by some that it was for this reason that Saddam Hussein had numerous murals painted all over Baghdad portraying himself as a Muslim Knight on a white horse with sword drawn doing valiant battle against the infidels.

It's interesting that Islamic tradition indicates the verse within the Bible that provides a sign for the Mahdi is the verse of Revelation 6:2. That verse is associated with the opening of the first seal within the book of Revelation as follows:

THE FIRST SEAL:

> Then a white horse appeared, and he who sat on it had a bow.
> A crown was given to him, and he came out conquering, and to
> conquer. ~ **Revelation 6:2**

Christians universally accept this Bible verse to signify the appearance of the antichrist. For Christians, the white color of this horse represents peace because the antichrist will rise to power by promising peace (the signing of the seven-year peace treaty with Israel). This first seal is opened at the beginning of the tribulation. The first three-and-a-half years of the tribulation will be marked by an appearance of peace, but the antichrist will ultimately bring war and destruction in the final three-and-a-half years of the tribulation period.[21] The weapon the rider carries is a bow. The bow typically represents some sort of offensive weapon in the Bible. Jesus is depicted as having a double-edged sword coming out of His mouth when He returns to earth. The double-edged sword represents truth, which is His word. The tool Jesus uses to defeat Satan and those attached to the world is simply speaking the truth of His word. The rider, depicted with a bow, comes with an offensive weapon. The tool he will use to try to convince people to come to him is an offensive weapon (pressure, manipulation, and coercion in a menacing way). We can be assured anyone coming to us in this type of manner is only trying to deceive us.

For Christians, the rider on this horse is representative of the antichrist. He will arrive with promises of peace and prosperity, but his message will be a false message and will be delivered in a coercive and manipulative way. The rider emerging from the first seal also signifies false gospels and false religions. This rider will not proclaim to believe in the crucifixion and resurrection of Jesus. He will not believe Jesus was the son of God. He will provide a message that is counter to the Christian gospel. He will present the religion of Islam and will demand the world convert to the true teachings of the Islamic faith. Within the book of Revelation, the seals that follow the emergence of this rider are summa-

---

[21]   Roger Barrier, "Opening the Seven Seals of Revelation", Preach It Teach It, September 10, 2021, *Gog and Magog: A Revelation from John Explained - Preach It Teach It*

rized as follows:[22]

- Peace is taken from the earth
- Famine
- Plagues and death
- Persecution and Martyrdom of God's people
- A great earthquake
- The wrath of God

There are other Islamic traditions that say the Mahdi will find or uncover secret ancient texts near the town of Antioch. It is said the ancient texts he will find will be presented to the world as uncorrupted sacred texts of the Torah that will refute the Jews. One Islamic tradition from Ka'b al-Ahbar says, "He will be called 'Mahdi" because he will guide (yahdi) to something hidden and will bring out the Torah and Gospel from a town called Antioch." Another Islamic tradition states, "he is called the Mahdi because he will guide the people to a mountain in Syria from which he will bring out the volumes of the Torah to refute the Jews. It is also said, at the hands of the Mahdi the Ark of the Covenant will be brought forth from the Lake of Tiberias and taken and placed in Jerusalem." And in another Islamic tradition, Ad-Dani says, "He is called the Mahdi because he will be guided to a mountain in Syria from which he will bring forth the volumes of the Torah with which to argue against the Jews and at his hands a group of them will become Muslim." Apparently, the purpose of finding these "lost" portions of the Old and New Testaments, as well as the Ark of the Covenant, will be to "help" the Mahdi win converts from both Christianity and Judaism prior to "eradicating" the remainder who do not convert to Islam.

There is Islamic tradition that states the Mahdi will conquer Israel. Islamic tradition pictures the Mahdi as joining with the army of Muslim warriors carrying black flags. The Mahdi will then lead this army to Israel and re-conquer it for Islam. The Jews will be slaughtered until very few remain, and Jerusalem will become the location of the Mahdi's rule over the Earth. One Islamic tradition states, "Armies carrying black flags will come from Khurasan. No power will be able to stop them, and they will finally reach Eela (Baitul Maqdas in Jerusalem) where they will erect

---

[22]   "Chapter Five Comparing The Biblical Antichrist and the Mahdi", Answering Islam, *https://www.answering-islam.org/Authors/JR/Future/ch05_comparing_the_biblical_antichrist.htm*

their flags." There is a very famous Islamic tradition that is often quoted throughout the Islamic world that speaks of the Mahdi's military campaign against Israel. The Prophet said, "The last hour would not come unless the Muslims will fight against the Jews and the Muslims would kill them until the Jews would hide themselves behind a stone or a tree and a stone or a tree would say: Muslim, or the servant of Allah, there is a Jew behind me; come and kill him".[23]

Another of the Antichrist's goals according to the Book of Daniel is said to be that he will "try to change the set times and the laws": He will speak against the Most High and oppress his saints and try to change the set times and the laws. The saints will be handed over to him for a time, times and half a time. Daniel 7:25 says, "He will speak words against the Most High, and will wear out the saints of the Most High. He will plan to change the times and the law; and they will be given into his hand until a time and times and half a time." It is said the antichrist will desire to change two things; times and laws. We have already seen the Mahdi will attempt to change the law by instituting the Islamic Shariah law all over the earth, but we have not seen any evidence in Islamic apocalyptic literature of him changing the "times." The simple question however is, who else other than a Muslim would desire to change the "times and laws"? Besides the Gregorian calendar used by the West, there is also a Jewish, a Hindu and a Muslim calendar among others. Jews or Hindus however are not a people who would desire to impose their religious laws or calendars onto the rest of the world. Islam, however, has both its own laws and its own calendar, both of which it would desire to impose onto the entire world. The Islamic calendar is based on the career of Muhammad. It begins at the migration (Hijra) of Muhammad from Mecca to Medina. The Muslim calendar is viewed as being mandatory for all to observe. Dr. Waleed Mahanna articulates the Islamic position regarding the Islamic "Hijra" Calendar: It is considered a divine command to use a (Hijra) calendar with 12 (purely) lunar months without intercalation, as evident from the Holy Qur'an. Not only does Islam view as a divine imperative the use of a unique religious calendar, it also has its own week.

Unlike the Western rhythm of a week, Monday through Friday being the body of the workweek followed by Saturday and Sunday as the

---

[23] "Chapter Four The Mahdi: Islam's Awaited Messiah", Answering Islam, *https://answering-islam.org/Authors/JR/Future/ch04_the_mahdi.htm*

weekend with Judaism and Christianity using these two days for their respective days of worship, Islam holds Friday as its sacred day of prayer. This is the day that Muslims meet at the Mosque to pray and listen to a sermon. Thus, it's completely plausible the Biblical reference to the Antichrist who will "try to change the set times and the laws" is a Muslim. As we look at the full picture, only Islam fits the bill of a system that has its own unique calendar and week based on its own religious history and a clear system of law that it wishes to impose onto the entire earth. Surely if a Muslim ever emerges who is as powerful as the Mahdi, he will certainly attempt to institute both the Islamic Law worldwide, and the Islamic calendar and week as well. [24]

A summary of all the Islamic attributes of the Mahdi are as follows:
- The Mahdi is Islam's primary Messiah figure.
- He will be a descendant of Muhammad and will bear Muhammad's name (Muhammad bin Abdullah).
- He will be a very devout Muslim.
- He will be an unparalleled spiritual, political and military world leader.
- He will emerge after a period of great turmoil and suffering upon the earth.
- He will establish justice and righteousness throughout the world and eradicate tyranny and oppression.
- He will be the Caliph and Imam (vice-regent and leader) of Muslims worldwide
- He will lead a world revolution and establish a new world order.
- He will lead military action against all those who oppose him.
- He will invade many countries.
- He will make a seven-year peace treaty with a Jew of priestly lineage.
- He will conquer Israel for Islam and lead the "faithful Muslims" in a final slaughter/battle against Jews.
- He will establish the new Islamic world headquarters from Jerusalem.
- He will rule for seven years.

---

[24] "Chapter Five Comparing The Biblical Antichrist and the Mahdi", Answering Islam, *https://www.answering-islam.org/Authors/JR/Future/ch05_comparing_the_biblical_antichrist.htm*

- He will cause Islam to be the only religion practiced on the earth.
- He will appear riding a white horse.
- He will discover some previously undiscovered biblical manuscripts that he will use to argue with the Jews and cause some Jews to convert to Islam.
- He will also re-discover the Ark of the Covenant from the Sea of Galilee, which he will bring to Jerusalem.
- He will have supernatural power from Allah over the wind and the rain and crops.
- He will possess and distribute enormous amounts of wealth.
- He will be loved by all the people of the earth.
- He will attempt to change the set times and laws.

I will point out the summarized characteristics of the Mahdi mirror those of the Christian antichrist. The Mahdi (the Islamic Messiah) embodies the full image of the Christian antichrist, and, in fact, the very Bible verse spoken about by both Christianity and Islam (in the book of Revelation) attribute the character as being the same individual. The Christian view of this individual is he will be the antichrist. The Islamic view of this same individual is he will be their messiah. The Bible is very clear that Satan, through the Antichrist, will specifically target first Jews, and then Christians for death. Revelation 12:1 says, "A great sign was seen in heaven: a woman clothed with the sun, and the moon under her feet, and on her head a crown of twelve stars." The woman identified within this Bible verse represents Israel. Then, Revelation 12:2-5 says, "She was with child. She cried out in pain, laboring to give birth. Another sign was seen in heaven. Behold, a great red dragon, having seven heads and ten horns, and on his heads seven crowns. His tail drew one third of the stars of the sky, and threw them to the earth. The dragon stood before the woman who was about to give birth, so that when she gave birth he might devour her child. She gave birth to a son, a male child, who is to rule all the nations with a rod of iron. Her child was caught up to God, and to his throne." This is a clear reference to Jesus, the Christian savior. The dragon is easily identified as Satan. We see in these Bible verses Satan desires to kill Jesus, but instead Jesus is, "snatched up to God and to his throne." This is a reference to Jesus' ascension to heaven after the resurrection (Acts 1:8). After this, Satan was hurled down to earth, and his angels with him. Satan pursued the woman who had given birth to the male child. The woman was given the two wings of a great eagle, so that she might fly to the place prepared for her in the desert, where she would be taken care of for a time, times and half a time, out of the serpent's reach. Then the dragon was enraged at the woman and went off to make war against the rest of her offspring—those who obey God's commandments and hold to the testimony of Jesus. Revelation 12:1-6,9,13,14,17 We see Satan is, "enraged at the woman (Israel) and went off to make war against the rest of her offspring--those who obey God's commandments and hold to the testimony of Jesus." Israel's "other offspring" are those Christians who indeed "obey God's commandments and hold to the testimony of Jesus." This is the only passage that makes specific reference to Satan making a direct target of both Jews and Christians together. And we know this passage is speaking specifically of the end-times, because it mentions twice the three-and-a-half year period (1,260 days and "a time, times and half a time"). The Antichrist will have authority to wage war against the saints: The beast was given a mouth to utter proud words and blasphemies and to exercise his authority for forty-two months. He opened his mouth to blaspheme God, and to slander his name and his dwelling place and those who live in heaven. He was given power to make war against the saints and to conquer them. And he was given authority over every tribe, people, language and nation. Revelation 13:5-7 says, " A mouth speaking great things and blasphemy was given to him. Authority to make war for forty-two months was given to him. He opened his mouth for blasphemy against God, to blaspheme his name, and his dwelling, those who dwell in heaven. It was given to him to make war with the saints, and to overcome them. Authority over every tribe, people, language, and nation was given to him." The prophet Daniel also saw that the Antichrist would have this authority to wage a successful war against "the saints". Saints is also translated as "holy ones" in some translations. It speaks primarily of the true followers of Jesus who know and serve the One True God. He will speak against the Most High and oppress his saints and try to change the set times and the laws. The saints will be handed over to him for a time, times and half a time. Daniel 7:25 says, "He will speak words against the Most High, and will wear out the saints of the Most High. He will plan to change the times and the law; and they will be given into his hand until a time and times and half a time." Again, we see the reference to the three-and-a-half-year period that Antichrist will persecute those who resist him.

The Bible is clear, the Antichrist will specifically target those who resist his attempts to establish his religion all over the earth. From the book of Revelation as well as the Prophet Daniel, we see the two groups Satan is most enraged against. They are the Jews and the Christians.[25] Interestingly enough, Islamic tradition speaks much of the Mahdi's special calling to convert Christians and Jews to Islam yet speaks very little specifically of conversions from other faiths. It appears converting Christians and Jews to Islam will be the primary evangelistic thrust of the Mahdi. The following quote from Ayatollah Ibrahim Amini clearly articulates this vision, "The Mahdi will offer the religion of Islam to the Jews and Christians; if they accept it, they will be spared, otherwise they will be killed."[26] There is a specific Islamic tradition spoken about the actions of the Mahdi that state he will, "Break the cross and kill the swine". When this tradition speaks of breaking the cross and killing the swine it is likely a reference that the Mahdi will attempt to contrast the arguments the Christians have against Islam (primarily that Jesus died on the cross and was resurrected by God).

I believe there will be some even within the Muslim community that will rebel against the Mahdi, not all within the Muslim community will believe the message of the Mahdi. This should not surprise us, as Christians, in the end the antichrist will demand the entire world worship him as a God. When he sets up an image of himself at God's holy temple in Jerusalem. Islam, at its core, believes in a God of heaven. They do not believe in the worship of any man. This is why they have a massive problem with Jesus being presented as the son of God, because by doing so He is being made equal to a God. There should be little surprise then there will be people even within the Muslim community when the end comes that will reject the antichrist (the Mahdi), and along with Christians and Jews, the Mahdi will also be killing Muslims that don't profess to believe in him as a Messiah or a God. I take this as a blessing because I think it provides evidence there may be many even within the Muslim communi-

---

[25] "Chapter Five Comparing The Biblical Antichrist and the Mahdi", Answering Islam, *https://www.answering-islam.org/Authors/JR/Future/ch05_comparing_the_biblical_antichrist.htm*

[26] "Chapter Five Comparing The Biblical Antichrist and the Mahdi", Answering Islam, *https://www.answering-islam.org/Authors/JR/Future/ch05_comparing_the_biblical_antichrist.htm*

ty that will eventually realize the man that is demanding to be worshiped may be a false Messiah. It also bears repeating the previous prophecy identified in this book that states the kingdom the antichrist will preside over will be a kingdom that is divided and does not stick together. The reason for this may be the fact that there may be some Muslims that reject the Mahdi's demand to be worshiped as the true Messiah and a God.

THE KINGDOM OF THE BEAST

A DESCRIPTION OF THE KINGDOM the beast will preside over is provided in the book of Daniel chapter 2. In speaking about this kingdom we are told the following, "The fourth kingdom will be strong as iron, because iron breaks in pieces and subdues all things; and as iron that crushes all these, it will break in pieces and crush. Whereas you saw the feet and toes, part of potters' clay, and part of iron, it will be a divided kingdom; but there will be in it the strength of the iron, because you saw the iron mixed with miry clay. As the toes of the feet were part of iron, and part of clay, so the kingdom will be partly strong, and partly broken. Whereas you saw the iron mixed with miry clay, they will mingle themselves with the seed of men; but they won't cling to one another, even as iron does not mix with clay." As a result, we can see this will be a divided kingdom characterized by internal strife. Revelation 13:1-10 provides another description of the kingdom the beast will preside over.

REVELATION 13:1-10:

Then I stood on the sand of the sea. I saw a beast coming up out of the sea, having ten horns and seven heads. On his horns were ten crowns, and on his heads, blasphemous names. The beast which I saw was like a leopard, and his feet were like those of a bear, and his mouth like the mouth of a lion. The dragon gave him his power, his throne, and great authority. One of his heads looked like it had been wounded fatally. His fatal wound was healed, and the whole earth marveled at the beast. They worshiped the dragon, because he gave his authority to the beast, and they worshiped the beast, saying, "Who is like the beast? Who is able to make war with him?" A mouth speaking great things and blasphemy was given to him. Authority to make war for forty-two months was given to him. He opened his mouth for blasphemy against God, to blaspheme his name, and his dwelling, those who dwell in heaven. It was given to him to make war with the saints, and to overcome them. Authority over every tribe, people, language, and nation was given to him. All who dwell on the earth will worship him, everyone whose name has not been written from the foundation of the world in the book of life of the Lamb who has been killed. If anyone has an ear, let him hear. If anyone is to go into captivity, he will go into captivity. If anyone is to be killed with the sword, he must be killed. Here is the endurance and the faith of the saints.

In reading these Bible verses we can see the kingdom the beast will preside over will be a conglomeration, or a confederation of nations with a confederation of kings or rulers that will be given some level of authority by the antichrist through Satan's power. We see evidence of this in Revelation 17 12-13 that says, "The ten horns that you saw are ten kings who have received no kingdom as yet, but they receive authority as kings with the beast for one hour. These have one mind, and they give their power and authority to the beast." We see the beast's kingdom rise out of the sea. The sea, in Biblical terms, carries a lot of symbolism with it. Typically, it represents chaos, disorder, the unknown, and non-Jewish nations. We can also see both the antichrist and the kingdom of the beast will be provided power by Satan (the dragon). Satan will empower the beast and his kingdom to do supernatural things. I believe this will include supernatural events, such as swallowing up an entire army in the desert to permit the Mahdi to rise to power. God will give authority over the antichrist and their kingdom to prevail over God's people for a finite period (42 months) to make war with them and kill them. It's important to note this authority is given to them by God. God permits the great deception to take place, and he presents an environment where it will appear the antichrist and his kingdom will be prevailing against God's chosen and holy people. Many people might ask why God would permit such a thing. How can a loving God allow such a thing to happen? How could God permit Satan to create such a convincing deception designed to even deceive God's elect if it were possible to do so? The answer to this question is provided in 2 Thessalonians 2:8-10.

2 THESSALONIANS 2:8-10:

Then the lawless one will be revealed, whom the Lord will kill with the breath of his mouth, and destroy by the manifestation of his coming; even he whose coming is according to the working of Satan with all power and signs and lying wonders, and with all deception of wickedness for those who are being lost, **because they didn't receive the love of the truth, that they might be saved.** [emphasis added]

The above Bible verse says those who will perish will be those that did not receive the love of the truth. Therefore, we can be assured there is only one protection and that is to receive the love of the truth. If you sincerely love the truth, that will protect you from this incredibly convincing deception. The word *love* here in this Bible verse, in Greek, is *agape*. This is a very strong word. It means a passionate devotion to the truth. It doesn't mean you just read your Bible once every day or go to a church that preaches the Bible, it means you *esteem* the truth above all else in your life. Lots of people who are called Bible believing Christians don't exhibit the love of the truth of God's word as it is meant in this Bible verse. There are two ways you can understand the truth. The truth is Jesus, and the truth is the word of God. I want to exhort you to love the Word of God *passionately*. To take more time with it than you take with your television set or any other activity. If you don't then I am afraid you are at risk of being deceived by the great deception God will allow Satan to create that is intended to deceive the world in the end times. It says in verse 11, *"For this reason God will send them strong delusion."* Have you ever thought about that? If you don't receive the love of truth and practice it, God will send you a strong delusion. If God sends you the delusion there is no way you can avoid it, you will be deceived. It'll be a judgment of God because of our failure to love and obey the truth.[27]

I have written this book to draw attention to the fact that during the end times God will permit a great deception to be provided to humanity, for those that don't know the actual truth provided within God's holy word they will be deceived by this deception. I pray for you, and I urge you as Bible believing Christians to truly commit yourselves to living the way God desires you to live, with Him at the very *center* of your life. Allow Him to *truly* be your lord, not just your savior. Spend time in God's word so you may understand it and so you may not be deceived by the great deception that will be provided to humanity during the end times.

I have provided reasons why I believe the antichrist will arise out of

---

[27]   "Islam-armageddon-end-times", AboutIslam, *https://aboutislam.net/counseling/ask-about-islam/islam-armageddon-end-times/*

the nation of Turkey. It's important to note the region of Turkey, specifically the area known as Anatolia was part of the Roman empire before the rise of Islam. The Roman public gained control as early as 129 BC and later became fully integrated into the Roman empire under Emperor Constantine, who established Constantinople (modern day Istanbul) as the new capital of the Eastern Roman empire. This is important because, as we know, the antichrist must arise out of a nation that was part of the Roman empire.[28] Further, I believe once the Mahdi has been identified most, if not all, Islamic nations will quickly pledge their allegiance to him. The major nations of the world that have a population where most of the population believe in the Mahdi and are looking for his appearance include the following:

- Turkey
- Iraq
- Syria
- Iran
- Afghanistan
- Tunisia
- Malasya
- Lebanon
- Pakistan
- Algeria
- Morocco

I believe the kingdom the beast will preside over will be formed from a conglomeration of these Islamic nations. It should be noted of all these nations Turkey is a bit unique. Turkey is 99% Muslim but only 16% of those Muslims would consider themselves to be "extremely religious". Turkey is the only nation of the above set of nations that has a headscarf ban. Turkey is the most moderate Muslim nation. This is because its laws are mostly not based on religion. Most other Arab nations have laws affected by Sharia, but this is not the case for Turkey. It's officially a secular nation. Some view Turkey as being like the United States in that it is a secular state and very moderate within the Muslim world. These differences between Turkey and these other Muslim nations may be the reason

---

28 "What does it mean that Babylon the Great has fallen (Revelation 18:2", Got Questions your questions, Biblical answers, *https://www.gotquestions.org/Babylon-the-Great-has-fallen.html*

the Bible says these nations won't cling to themselves but there will be internal battles and internal conflicts within the kingdom of the beast. I believe another obvious reason these nations won't be able to cling together is they will essentially be led by Satan. Satan has never been a king. As a result, Satan won't be able to lead as a true king would, like Jesus. He won't be able to truly unify this group of nations under his leadership because he is not the true king. Jesus is the true king!

I believe at some point this internal conflict may cause an assassination attempt against the antichrist. The above Bible verses tell us, one of his heads looked like it had been wounded fatally. His fatal wound was healed, and the whole earth marveled at the beast. They worshiped the dragon, because he gave his authority to the beast, and they worshiped the beast, saying, 'Who is like the beast? Who can make war with him?'" You can see the beast will be permitted to grow exceedingly strong through deceptions and miraculous signs God permits Satan to perform. Upon the assassination attempt it will seem to the world as if the antichrist miraculously recovered (was miraculously healed in a supernatural manner). This will only add to the deception that will be permitted to be played out by God against humanity during the end times. It's important we all read God's word and really meditate on it. We need to try to understand what it means, and what truth God wants to convey to us. We can discern this truth through diligent study of His word, prayers for wisdom, and listening to the prompting of the Holy Spirit.

THE FALSE PROPHET

MATTHEW 24:15-27 WARNS US OF false prophets as we approach the end times. Further, the Bible explains that many false prophets will come in the name of God and will even present themselves to be the true Messiah.

> When, therefore, you see the abomination of desolation, which was spoken of through Daniel the prophet, standing in the holy place (let the reader understand), then let those who are in Judea flee to the mountains. Let him who is on the housetop not go down to take out the things that are in his house. Let him who is in the field not return back to get his clothes. But woe to those who are with child and to nursing mothers in those days! Pray that your flight will not be in the winter nor on a Sabbath, for then there will be great suffering, such as has not been from the beginning of the world until now, no, nor ever will be. Unless those days had been shortened, no flesh would have been saved. But for the sake of the chosen ones, those days will be short-ened. Then if any man tells you, 'Behold, here is the Christ!' or, 'There!' don't believe it. For there will arise false Christ's, and false prophets, and they will show great signs and wonders, so as to lead astray, if possible, even the chosen ones. Behold, I have told you beforehand. If therefore they tell you, 'Behold, he is in the wilderness,' don't go out; or 'Behold, he is in the inner rooms,' don't believe it. For as the lightning flashes from the east, and is seen even to the west, so will the coming of the Son of Man be.~ **Matthew 24:15-27**

There is one false prophet, in particular, however that will act in tan-dem with the antichrist. He will be subservient to the antichrist, but He will deliver a message that the world should worship the antichrist. He will support the antichrist and will be provided special abilities to per-form miracles such as bringing fire down from the sky to deceive people into worshiping the antichrist. This false prophet is described in Revela-tion chapter 13:11-18.

I saw another beast coming up out of the earth. He had two horns like a lamb, and he spoke like a dragon. He exercises all the authority of the first beast in his presence. He makes the earth and those who dwell in it worship the first beast, whose fatal wound was healed. **He performs great signs, even making fire come down out of the sky to the earth in the sight of people.** *[emphasis added]* He deceives my own people who dwell on the earth because of the signs he was granted to do in front of the beast, saying to those who dwell on the earth that they should make an image to the beast who had the sword wound and lived. It was given to him to give breath to it, to the image of the beast, that the image of the beast should both speak, and cause as many as wouldn't worship the image of the beast to be killed. He causes all, the small and the great, the rich and the poor, and the free and the slave, to be given marks on their right hands, or on their foreheads; and that no one would be able to buy or to sell, unless he has that mark, which is the name of the beast or the number of his name. Here is wisdom. He who has understanding, let him calculate the number of the beast, for it is the number of a man. His number is six hundred sixty-six." ~ *[emphasis added]* **Revelation 13:11-18**

We can see within the pages of the Bible there is an unholy partnership between the antichrist and the false prophet. From these Bible verses, we can determine a few things about the false prophet. First, he is called a beast - he is, like the Antichrist, a man possessed by Satan. He is another human pawn of the dragon (Satan), exercising the will of the dragon on earth. But instead of ten horns, he only has two. The horns speak of authority. The power and authority of the false prophet is clear, but it is not nearly equal to that of the Antichrist who is said to have ten horns. We also see the false prophet as a miracle worker. Among the many miracles he is said to have the ability to do, one is mentioned specifically: He is said to cause fire to come down from the sky. The false prophet's primary reason for performing miraculous signs is to cause the inhabitants of the earth to follow and even worship the Antichrist. The two are pictured as a team, a partnership with one common goal - deception, seduction and a luring away of anyone who worships Yahweh, the

God of the Bible.[29]

What I find truly interesting is Islam also describes an alignment between the Mahdi and an individual that they identify to be Jesus. Islam traditions state Jesus will return as a great prophet in the end times. In the Islamic traditions we find both the Mahdi and the Muslim Jesus. We also see, as in the case of the Antichrist and the false prophet, one is clearly filling a supporting role while the other is the leader. While the Mahdi is clearly described as being, "the Viceregent (Caliph) of Allah," The Muslim version of Jesus is one who will "espouse the cause of the Mahdi" and "follow him."[30] Instead of espousing the "cause" of the Father (Which is what the Christian Jesus did), the Muslim Jesus espouses the cause of the Mahdi. Instead of saving those followers of His whom the Father has placed under his oversight, the Muslim Jesus will slaughter those who remain faithful to the words of Jesus as found in the Christian Bible. The Muslim Jesus is not the tender strong shepherd of the gospels, but rather the wolf himself in the shepherd's clothing.

In Revelation 13:15 the Bible also says the false prophet will be given power to give breath to the image of the first beast (the antichrist), so it could speak and cause all who refused to worship the image to be killed. The image itself will have the ability to enforce the law of the false prophet; it will have the ability to cause people to be killed. This seems to work in tangent with the infamous "mark of the beast" that is part of the false prophet's system. All the inhabitants of the earth will be forced to receive a mark on his right hand or on his forehead, so that no one could buy or sell unless he had the mark, which is the name of the beast or the number of his name." (Revelation 13:17). As a result, we also see that the false prophet has a role of being the enforcer of the Antichrist's global worship movement. Imagine for a moment, a miracle working evangelist who is completely possessed by Satan and refuses to take no for an answer at the threat of death. This is exactly what the false prophet will be.

In Islamic tradition it says the Islamic Jesus will seek to convert both

---

29   "Chapter Seven Comparing the false prophet and the Muslim Jesus", Answering Islam, *https://answering-islam.org/Authors/JR/Future/ch07_comparing_the_false_prophet.htm*

30   "Chapter Seven Comparing the false prophet and the Muslim Jesus", Answering Islam, *https://answering-islam.org/Authors/JR/Future/ch07_comparing_the_false_prophet.htm*

Christians and Jews into a new religion (the pure form of the Islam religion that they will present to the world). Islamic tradition states when the Islamic Jesus comes, he will, "correct the misrepresentations and misinterpretations about himself. He will affirm the true message that he brought in his time as a prophet, and that he never claimed to be the Son of God. Furthermore, he will reaffirm in his second coming what he prophesied in his first coming bearing witness to the seal of the Messengers, Prophet Muhammad. In his second coming many non-Muslims will accept Jesus as a servant of Allah Almighty, as a Muslim and a member of the Community of Muhammad."[31] In addition, the Islamic Jesus will abolish the Jizyah tax, which is a tax paid by Christians or Jews in Muslim countries for protection. It is said when the Islamic Jesus abolishes this tax, he will leave Christians and Jews worldwide with only two options: convert to Islam or die. A specific Islamic tradition states, "Jesus, the son of Mary will soon descend among the Muslims as a just judge. Jesus will, therefore, judge according to the law of Islam. all people will be required to embrace Islam and there will be no other alternative." We can see here the biblical false prophet and the Muslim Jesus are both described as establishing a system of law that will enforce the mass execution of anyone who refuses to convert to the new global religion.

Finally, according to Islamic tradition, the Islamic Jesus will kill an entity known as the Dajjal. The Dajjal is essentially the Islamic antichrist. Islamic traditions paint a picture of the Islamic Jesus as being the leader of a great army that will "slaughter tens of thousands of Jews who are all said to be followers of the Dajjal." In these traditions the Jews are said to be his main followers. These Islamic traditions say the Islamic Jesus will "kill the Dajjal at the Gate of Hudd, near an Israeli airport, in the valley of 'Ifiq.'" The final war between the Jews will ensue, and the Muslims will be victorious and kill the Jews until "even a stone or a tree would say: Come here, Muslim, there is a Jew hiding behind me; kill him."

Muslims are awaiting a man to come that will claim to be the returned prophet Jesus. He will claim, according to Islamic tradition, he has been alive in heaven for the past two thousand years. He will claim he has been waiting to return to complete his life and accomplish his

---

[31] "Chapter Seven Comparing the false prophet and the Muslim Jesus", Answering Islam, *https://answering-islam.org/Authors/JR/Future/ch07_comparing_the_false_prophet.htm*

mission on earth. His message will be that he never died and was never resurrected by God. The Islamic Jesus will share many similarities of the Christian false prophet. In addition, the Islamic Dajjal may be viewed as a representation of the Christian Jesus Christ upon his second return to earth, as it is He that will be leading the army of the Jews the Islamic Jesus is said to kill. Again, this provides evidence of the great deception that will be permitted by God to play out during the final days which will lead many to be deceived.

Those being deceived will have their traditions that back up their faith. They will see miraculous signs and wonders that seem to verify the traditions they have believed in their entire lives. To them, it will seem as if things are playing out *exactly* as they would expect them to according to the traditions of their faith. What we can see is by permitting this great deception God is giving mankind a choice to make, to believe in the true gospel message, or believe in what will be a very convincing lie created and propagated by Satan. A lie crafted by Satan and yet empowered by God to deceive even the elect if it were possible to do so. This is the reason we must read and understand God's word. We must know God's word and meditate upon it so we can be equipped to see through the very convincing deception that will be playing out on the world stage in these final days.

THE FALL OF BABYLON THE GREAT

IN THE BOOK OF REVELATION, the Bible refers to Babylon the Great as a prostitute. Using the term prostitute within the Bible generally refers to a false religion, or a belief or spiritual message that leads people away from God's holy truth. The above Bible verse is clear. The beast will seek to destroy a great city known as Babylon the Great. The beast will also seek to destroy the great prostitute, which is a false religion. I believe the beast will be waging war against all religions on the face of the planet at the time of the destruction of Babylon the Great. It is a vivid picture, worth reading in its entirety:

REVELATION CHAPTER 18: THE FALL OF BABYLON THE GREAT

After these things, I saw another angel coming down out of the sky, having great authority. The earth was illuminated with his glory. He cried with a mighty voice, saying, "Fallen, fallen is Babylon the great, and she has become a habitation of demons, a prison of every unclean spirit, and a prison of every unclean and hateful bird! For all the nations have drunk of the wine of the wrath of her sexual immorality, the kings of the earth committed sexual immorality with her, and the merchants of the earth grew rich from the abundance of her luxury."

WARNING TO ESCAPE BABYLON'S JUDGMENT

I heard another voice from heaven, saying, "Come out of her, my people, that you have no participation in her sins, and that you don't receive of her plagues, for her sins have reached to the sky, and God has remembered her iniquities. Return to her just as she returned, and repay her double as she did, and according to her works. In the cup which she mixed, mix to her double. However much she glorified herself, and grew wanton, so much give her of torment and mourning. For she says in her heart, 'I sit a queen, and am no widow, and will in no way see mourning.'

Therefore, in one day her plagues will come: death, mourning, and famine; and she will be utterly burned with fire; for the Lord God who has judged her is strong."

THREEFOLD WOE OVER BABYLON'S FALL:

The kings of the earth who committed sexual immorality and lived wantonly with her will weep and wail over her, when they look at the smoke of her burning, standing far away for the fear of her torment, saying, 'Woe, woe, the great city, Babylon, the strong city! For your judgment has come in one hour.' The merchants of the earth weep and mourn over her, for no one buys their merchandise any more: merchandise of gold, silver, precious stones, pearls, fine linen, purple, silk, scarlet, all expensive wood, every vessel of ivory, every vessel made of most precious wood, and of brass, and iron, and marble; and cinnamon, incense, perfume, frankincense, wine, olive oil, fine flour, wheat, sheep, horses, chariots, and people's bodies and souls. The fruits which your soul lusted after have been lost to you. All things that were dainty and sumptuous have perished from you, and you will find them no more at all. The merchants of these things, who were made rich by her, will stand far away for the fear of her torment, weeping and mourning, saying, 'Woe, woe, the great city, she who was dressed in fine linen, purple, and scarlet, and decked with gold and precious stones and pearls! For in an hour such great riches are made desolate.' Every ship master, and everyone who sails anywhere, and mariners, and as many as gain their living by sea, stood far away, and cried out as they looked at the smoke of her burning, saying, 'What is like the great city?' They cast dust on their heads, and cried, weeping and mourning, saying, 'Woe, woe, the great city, in which all who had their ships in the sea were made rich by reason of her great wealth!' For she is made desolate in one hour. "Rejoice over her, O heaven, you saints, apostles, and prophets; for God has judged your judgment on her."

THE FINALITY OF BABYLON'S DOOM:

> A mighty angel took up a stone like a great millstone and cast it into the sea, saying, "Thus with violence will Babylon, the great city, be thrown down, and will be found no more at all. The voice of harpists, minstrels, flute players, and trumpeters will be heard no more at all in you. No craftsman, of whatever craft, will be found any more at all in you. The sound of a mill will be heard no more at all in you. The light of a lamp will shine no more at all in you. The voice of the bridegroom and of the bride will be heard no more at all in you; for your merchants were the princes of the earth; for with your sorcery all the nations were deceived. In her was found the blood of prophets and of saints, and of all who have been slain on the earth."

Later, Revelation returns to this theme, indicating the city will be destroyed at the hands of the beast. Evidence is provided in the following Bible verses from Revelation 17:

> The ten horns which you saw, and the beast, these will hate the prostitute, will make her desolate, will strip her naked, will eat her flesh, and will burn her utterly with fire. For God has put in their hearts to do what he has in mind, to be of one mind, and to give their kingdom to the beast, until the words of God should be accomplished. The woman whom you saw is the great city, which reigns over the kings of the earth." ~ **Revelation 17: 16-18**

The Bible makes it clear the antichrist will seek to destroy Babylon the Great, the great prostitute. At this time, I believe the antichrist will also seek to destroy all religions including God's elect people. The famine of God's word will likely occur during this time as the antichrist would seek to snuff out all Biblical scripture from the face of the planet. The antichrist will attempt to stop all religious practices and will try to completely snuff out the word of God (if it were possible to do). Amos speaks of a famine of God's word:

> Behold, the days come," says the Lord Yahweh, "that I will send a famine in the land, not a famine of bread, nor a thirst for water, but of hearing Yahweh's words. They will wander from sea to sea,

> and from the north even to the east; they will run back and forth
> to seek Yahweh's word, and will not find it."° ~ **Amos 8:11-12**

And Revelation encourages believers to separate themselves from this wickedness:

> I heard another voice from heaven, saying, "**Come out of her,
> my people, that you have no participation in her sins, and
> that you don't receive of her plagues.**" *[emphasis added]* ~ **Rev-
> elation 18:4**

From these verses we can see God will draw a distinction between the righteous and unrighteous when he permits the destruction of Babylon the Great. We can see God doesn't want His true believers to participate in the plagues He will allow to be unleashed on Babylon the Great, the great prostitute. The persecution by the beast on all religions on the face of the planet will be severe. The above Bible verses show God will make a distinction between His believers and others who follow false religions, but we can expect the persecution to be severe for all religions. Those following God will need to trust in Him during this time of great persecution.

The Bible doesn't provide clear evidence of the city that will be known as Babylon the Great. There has been much speculation about the identity of the city, but the Bible doesn't provide any clear indication. I think, however, there may be a clue provided for the identity of this city within Islamic tradition. There are many Islamic traditions that speak about the conquest of Constantinople (current day Istanbul), and many within the Islamic faith will verify the conquest of Constantinople was fulfilled in 1453 when it fell to Islamic powers. The Islamic conquest of Constantinople can't be overstated in terms of its importance to Islam. The fall of this city has been described as producing the most seismic disruption that happened in medieval history. The fall of Constantinople signified the end of the Roman empire and the conquest of Islam over the Byzantine Roman empire. After the fall of the city, it was renamed to its current name of Istanbul.

Within Islamic tradition, however, there are other traditions that state the conquest of Constantinople will take place towards the end of times, when the Dijjal is just around the corner, when the Mahdi is on the world stage. Within these Islamic traditions it is also stated the city will fall in a miraculous manner, without bloodshed.[32] This Islamic tradition states, "You will fight Constantinople three times. The first time you will do well but you will not succeed. The second time you will enter into Sulah with the Constantinople so much so that Masjid will be built inside Constantinople. Then you will return for a third time, and you will conquer it with the 'Takbir'. You will say Allahu Akbar and it will be conquered. And the prophet said one third of the city will be destroyed, one third will burn down, and one third will be divided amongst you." A second Islamic tradition concerning the conquest of this city states, "Have you heard of a city half of which is in the water and half of which is in the land? The Qiyama will not happen until 70,000 of the Bani Ishaq will conquer it. Not the Bani Ismail. The Bani Ishaq will conquer it. and when they come to it, they, the Bani Ishaq will not fight with swords, nor will they fight with arrows, rather they will say La Ilaha Ill Allah Allahu Akbar and one of the sides will fall down then they will say that again and another side will fall down, then they will say it again and again until all four sides have fallen down. Then they will enter the city and begin to distribute Ghanim and while they are distributing the Ghanim a Shaytan will call, or a crier will call that verily the Dajjal has come out to your family, and they will leave everything and return to their family."[33]

In trying to interpret this second Islamic tradition about the conquest of Constantinople that will take place at the end times it is important to understand who the Bani Ishaq might be. Some have identified them as 70,000 "converts". They will have "converted" and will be fighting on the side of the Muslims. It is at the hands of these "converts" that the city will fall. The city will not fall at the hands of the "born" Muslims. It will be conquered by those who are pure. Those who have chosen to fight with the truth. It is said that Allah will bless them, and when they say the Takbir it will cause the walls of the city to come down, and they will then conquer the city.[34]

These two Islamic traditions would seem to point to the destruction

---

[32]   "The Final Days Series, The Rise of the Turks predicted over 1400 years ago", YouTube, *https://www.youtube.com/watch?v=7qffoAibQd8*

[33]   "The Final Days Series, The Rise of the Turks predicted over 1400 years ago", YouTube, *https://www.youtube.com/watch?v=7qffoAibQd8*

[34]   "The Final Days Series, The Rise of the Turks predicted over 1400 years ago", YouTube, *https://www.youtube.com/watch?v=7qffoAibQd8*

of current day Istanbul at the hands of Muslims (at the hands of the Beast), during the great tribulation period. The timing of the conquest of this city would seem to align with the timing of the destruction of Babylon the Great. As a result, it may provide evidence the city that will fall during the end times which the Bible identifies as Babylon the Great might be Istanbul. This is only a guess on my part based upon what I see in Islamic traditions, but we have seen evidence previously where some of the Islamic traditions that speak about the events of the end times mirror in many ways, or are the same event taken from the opposite point of view. As a result, we can't dismiss the coincidence that Islamic tradition calls for the destruction of a major city during the end times, and this city might represent Babylon the Great.

THE HOLY HIGHWAY AND TRIBULATION TEMPLE

ISAIAH 11:16: THE HOLY HIGHWAY

There will be a highway for the remnant that is left of his people from Assyria, like there was for Israel in the day that he came up out of the land of Egypt.

ISAIAH 19:23-25: THE HOLY HIGHWAY

In that day there will be a highway out of Egypt to Assyria, and the Assyrian shall come into Egypt, and the Egyptian into Assyria; and the Egyptians will worship with the Assyrians. In that day, Israel will be the third with Egypt and with Assyria, a blessing within the earth; because Yahweh of Armies has blessed them, saying, "Blessed be Egypt my people, Assyria the work of my hands, and Israel my inheritance."

ISAIAH 35:8-10

A highway will be there, a road, and it will be called "The Holy Way". The unclean shall not pass over it, but it will be for those who walk in the Way. Wicked fools shall not go there. No lion will be there, nor will any ravenous animal go up on it. They will not be found there; but the redeemed will walk there. Then Yahweh's ransomed ones will return and come with singing to Zion; and everlasting joy will be on their heads. They will obtain gladness and joy, and sorrow and sighing will flee away.

Notice the term "remnant" In Isaiah 11:16. This highway would seem to represent a reunion between God and the remaining remnant of His people. This prophetic Bible verse speaks of the remnant population of Israel during the tribulation period. His people will be instrumental in bringing salvation to Egypt and Assyria. I would argue other gentile nations of the world will be witnessed to as well during this time. Many in those nations will also repent and turn to God. Further, the highway represents a spiritual highway rather than an actual highway. The point of the prophecy is God will remove all obstacles. He will smooth the way for His people to turn to Him. This includes both Jew and Gentile. Three nations have been included here (Assyria, Egypt, and Israel). Assyria and Egypt are pagan (Gentile) nations, while Israel represents God's chosen nation. This is, perhaps, the highway people will use to come to Jerusalem to take part in the Festival of Tabernacles after the Gog/Magog war.

This same highway may be used for the population of the ten northern tribes to return to their ancestral homeland of Israel. The Bible says they will be drawn back to their ancestral homeland of Israel following the wars fought in Israel. The Bible uses the three nations of Israel, Egypt, and Assyria to signify true believers will turn toward God, and many of these believers may come from Gentile, or pagan, nations. Furthermore, it uses Israel in the context of these Bible verses to show Israel, as God's chosen nation, will be instrumental in leading many from these other nations back toward God. God used Assyria to destroy the northern nation of Israel. Assyria's destruction of Israel scattered the ten northern tribes throughout the world and much of the population of the original ten northern tribes of Israel remain scattered today. It is this population that had been scattered that will be drawn back to their ancestral homeland during the tribulation period.

The holy highway includes three key characteristics:
- The highway is reserved for only the righteous in God's sight.
- The highway is a place of safety (No Lion or ravenous beast will be there).
- The highway is a place of joy.

What I take from the prophetic Bible verses above is they speak to the creation of a holy highway between gentile nations and Israel. God secures a safe path for many to repent and turn to Him. If we seek God earnestly, He will make a way for us to find Him. The Bible spells out this highway will be a place of joy. This leads me to conclude that even during the darkest of times of the tribulation period there will be joy for God's true believers. We know the final three-and-a-half years of the Great Tribulation will be terrible. I find encouragement knowing God says there will be joy on the highway. We can celebrate that fact!

God is love. He will always make a way for His followers to come to Him or repent and turn to Him. If you are looking for a savior, why not look to the Lord? He promises to clear all barriers for you to come to Him and seek your salvation.

> "Behold, I stand at the door and knock. If anyone hears my voice and opens the door, then I will come in to him, and will dine with him, and he with me." ~ **Revelation 3:20**

God will clear every barrier for you to come to Him. He will make the path as easy as possible for you to follow. There is joy in accepting Jesus as your savior. There is great joy in walking the path He has laid out for your unique purpose in His kingdom. My earnest prayer for you is for you to accept His offer of salvation, and then for you to start walking down the path that He has laid out for you as your role to play in His story.

THE TRIBULATION TEMPLE:

> A reed like a rod was given to me. Someone said, "Rise, and measure God's temple, and the altar, and those who worship in it. Leave out the court which is outside of the temple, and don't measure it, for it has been given to the nations. They will tread the holy city under foot for forty-two months." ~ **Revelation 11:1-2**

The act of measuring is a sign of God's ownership. The above Bible verse is prophetic because it speaks to rebuilding the temple during the tribulation period. It will take place when permission is granted to Israel to rebuild the temple by the antichrist. I believe the timing of this might be shortly after the Gog/Magog war. The outer courtyard is excluded from this measurement because the antichrist will demand to be worshiped as the Messiah in the outer courtyard of the temple. During the first half of the tribulation period worship will again be permitted. During the second half of the tribulation, the antichrist will desecrate the temple by setting up an image (or statue) to be worshiped. He will put an end to the sacrifices being made there. He will demand to be worshiped as the Messiah. This is the betrayal and abomination spoken about in the Great Tribulation.

THE MARK OF THE BEAST

The mark of the beast will take place during the great tribulation period. A portion of the Jewish nation of Israel will realize they have entered a treaty with the antichrist and many Jews will flee to the wilderness to seek God's protection. Some Jews will be persecuted by the antichrist, but some will be able to escape. God asks John to count those worshipers in the Temple. This signifies God's protection over His people. During the great tribulation God will protect those who faithfully worship Him. He will make a distinction between His followers and the wicked who choose to continue to follow the worldly leader (antichrist) and take the mark of the beast.

TWO HOLY WITNESSES

GOD WILL PROVIDE TWO HOLY witnesses to Israel during the time of the Great Tribulation. The two holy witnesses will be revealed at some point during the tribulation period. I believe the two holy witnesses will lead Israel into the place prepared for them in the wilderness for their protection. They will be protected by God for three-and-a-half years to enable them to deliver a message of repentance to the earth. The antichrist will try to kill them, but he will be unable to do so for the period that God's protection remains on them.

> I will give power to my two witnesses, and they will prophesy one thousand two hundred sixty days, clothed in sackcloth." These are the two olive trees and the two lamp stands, standing before the Lord of the earth. If anyone desires to harm them, fire proceeds out of their mouth and devours their enemies. If anyone desires to harm them, he must be killed in this way. These have the power to shut up the sky, so that it may not rain during the days of their prophecy. They have power over the waters, to turn them into blood, and to strike the earth with every plague, as often as they desire.

THE WITNESSES KILLED

> When they have finished their testimony, the beast that comes up out of the abyss will make war with them, and overcome them, and kill them. Their dead bodies will be in the street of the great city, which spiritually is called Sodom and Egypt, where also their Lord was crucified. From among the peoples, tribes, languages, and nations, people will look at their dead bodies for three-and-a-half days and will not allow their dead bodies to be laid in a tomb. Those who dwell on the earth rejoice over them, and they will be glad. They will give gifts to one another, because these two prophets tormented those who dwell on the earth.

THE WITNESSES RESURRECTED

> After the three-and-a-half days, the breath of life from God entered them, and they stood on their feet. Great fear fell on those who saw them. I heard a loud voice from heaven saying to them, "Come up here!" They went up into heaven in the cloud, and their enemies saw them." ~ **Revelation 11:3-12**

At the time these two holy witnesses will be delivering their message of repentance to the earth, most of the world will still accept the beast's demand to be worshipped as the Messiah. This is because the mark of the beast will be in effect at that time and those that refuse to worship the beast and accept his mark will not be able to earn a living or purchase anything. They will be outcasts from society with no apparent means of supporting their families.

The story of Shadrach, Meshach, and Abednego serves as a perfect example to anyone that may be asked in the future to worship the beast during the times of the Great Tribulation. In Revelation we are told the false prophet will demand the population of the earth worship the beast as the messiah. I pray if I were ever faced with this demand my reaction would be like that of Shadrach, Meshach, and Abednego. You see, when they refused to bow and worship the statue, they were told they would be thrown into the furnace. Their reaction was simply to say whatever the king wanted to do was okay with them. They said they would not worship the statue. They didn't test their God. Instead, what they said was essentially they could not worship the idol because they served the one true living God. They said their God was powerful enough to save them. They also said even if their God chose not to save them, they would not bow down to the idol. They certainly made the king aware their God was powerful enough to save them, but they didn't demand it of their God. They simply said. Their God had the power to save them, but even if He didn't save them, they wouldn't bow and worship the idol. What a courageous response to the demand to bow and worship an idol!

> Shadrach, Meshach, and Abednego answered the king, "Nebuchadnezzar, we have no need to answer you in this matter. If it happens, our God whom we serve is able to deliver us from the burning fiery furnace; and he will deliver us out of your hand, O king. But if not, let it be known to you, O king, that we will not

serve your gods or worship the golden image which you have set up." ~ **Daniel 3:16-18**

During the last three-and-a-half years of the Great Tribulation we will be witness to many great signs and wonders. These signs and wonders will be performed by the false prophet (who will perform miraculous signs empowered by Satan and permitted by God), and the two holy witnesses who will be provided the ability to perform many miraculous signs. It will be really confusing for those that do not know their Bible to know who to believe in, but the Bible makes it clear. We are to only trust in Jesus. We are to test every miraculous sign by testing the testimony of the entity performing the sign. We are to test the entity to see if they profess to believe in the crucifixion and resurrection of Jesus. We are only to trust those that profess to believe in the crucifixion and resurrection of Jesus. We are not to trust any miraculous signs performed by anyone else. The message of the two holy witnesses will be to draw the inhabitants of the unrepentant population of the earth to turn to God and repent. We must understand that even in Egypt during the time of Moses some of the signs Moses performed were able to be replicated by Pharaoh's magicians. I believe the Bible communicates this to us to show we can't trust every miraculous sign we see. We must test who is delivering the sign to determine if the sign is coming from God or is being performed through dark arts and demons.

The magicians of Egypt did the same thing with their enchantments. So Pharaoh's heart was hardened, and he didn't listen to them, as Yahweh had spoken. ~ **Exodus 7:22**

We should expect the false prophet to be able to perform similar signs as those performed by Pharaoh's magicians in the book of Exodus (and even greater signs than those). The beast will attempt to kill the two holy witnesses, but they will be protected by God for three-and-a-half years. After the three-and-a-half years of God's protection has passed, the beast will be permitted, by God, to kill the two holy witnesses. This will take place only after their testimony is complete. This event will occur toward the end of the Great Tribulation.

When the dragon saw that he was thrown down to the earth, he persecuted the woman who gave birth to the male child. Two

> wings of the great eagle were given to the woman, that she might fly into the wilderness to her place, so that she might be nourished for a time, and times, and half a time, from the face of the serpent. ~ **Revelation 12:13-14**

The Bible verse above says the woman (Israel) is provided two great wings from an Eagle. She escapes (or at least some remnant of Israel escapes) to the wilderness to a place prepared for her. Israel will be protected from the dragon (Satan) for three-and-a-half years (the second half of the tribulation). These two great wings from an Eagle may represent Israel's two holy witnesses arriving during this time of the Great Tribulation. As a result, we can see these two holy witnesses are likely to come out of the remnant of Israel (true believers). They will be God's witnesses to the world for the period that God's divine protection is on them.

Then he said, "These are the two anointed ones who stand by the Lord of the whole earth." Zechariah 4:14

We can see these two holy witnesses were prophesized in the above Bible verse from Zechariah. This statement seems to be a continuation of a prophecy God gave the prophet Zechariah to show God accomplishes things through the power of His Spirit.

> He said to me, "What do you see?" I said, "I have seen, and behold, a lamp stand all of gold, with its bowl on the top of it, and its seven lamps on it; there are seven pipes to each of the lamps, which are on the top of it; and two olive trees by it, one on the right side of the bowl, and the other on the left side of it." I answered and spoke to the angel who talked with me, saying, "What are these, my lord?" Then the angel who talked with me answered me, "Don't you know what these are?" I said, "No, my lord. Then he answered and spoke to me, saying, "This is Yahweh's word to Zerubbabel, saying, 'Not by might, nor by power, but by my Spirit,' says Yahweh of Armies. Who are you, great mountain? Before Zerubbabel you are a plain; and he will bring out the capstone with shouts of 'Grace, grace, to it!'" Moreover, Yahweh's word came to me, saying, "The hands of Zerubbabel have laid the foundation of this house. His hands shall also finish it; and you will know that Yahweh of Armies has sent me to you. Indeed, who despises the day of small things? For these seven shall rejoice and shall see the plumb line in the hand of Zerubba-

bel. These are Yahweh's eyes, which run back and forth through the whole earth." ~ **Zechariah 4:2-10**

Olive oil symbolizes God's Holy Spirit. God encouraged Zerubbabel, the one who led the rebuilding of the temple, to remember spiritual things would be accomplished by God's Spirit. They would not be accomplished by his own doing (verse 6). After explaining this important principal about how His work is to be done, God returned to the vision of the olive trees Zechariah witnessed. The two olive trees represent God's two holy witnesses.

In Revelation 11 God reveals these two witnesses again, who will be full of God's Holy Spirit to do His work. They will arise prior to Christ's return to fulfil their ministry as a light to the world. As God pointed out to Zerubbabel, He accomplished things through the power of His Holy Spirit. He will do the same through His two witnesses during the Great Tribulation. The two witnesses will be speaking the truth of God's holy word at this time as they attempt to witness to humanity against the false prophet and the beast. The provision of the two holy witnesses during the Great Tribulation period shows even when things are at their darkest God provides His message to the earth. He provides His message of repentance to turn the unrepentant population towards Him. It is humanity's choice to determine if they want to hear and follow the message of repentance or to ignore the message of repentance and continue to turn away from their one true God. God is faithful. He will deliver His message to the ends of the earth even during the times of the Great Tribulation when all His believers will be hiding within the wilderness.

PETRA

WE MUST ALWAYS BE AWARE that even when the situation seems hopeless, God is able to provide an escape and a refuge. God will protect us. We can fully rely upon Him in the darkest of days. The Bible illustrates this by telling us what will happen when the antichrist defiles His holy temple and sets himself up in the temple to demand to be worshiped as the messiah. God gives clear instructions in the Bible to true believers. They should flee to the wilderness. They are to take nothing with them. This will be like the Israelites fleeing Egypt in the days of the Exodus. The Israelites fled Egypt with unleavened bread because they didn't have enough time to add yeast to their dough. We are instructed in the book of Revelation to flee without even going into our house to grab a cloak. We must have confidence God will rescue, protect, shelter, and nourish us in the wilderness as He did for the Israelites that fled Egypt. We must trust God's ability to care for us in a miraculous manner at the time when all else seems hopelessly lost. The second half of the tribulation will be ushered in when the antichrist demands to be worshiped at the temple, and he stops all sacrifices at the tribulation temple. Jews are directed to flee to the wilderness. The fleeing Jews will likely flee toward Edom (present day Jordan) in Biblical Bozrah where God has prepared a place of refuge for them. The place prepared to protect the Jews is Petra.[35] God may even nourish them with manna there, as in the days of Moses.

> The woman fled into the wilderness, where she has a place prepared by God, that there they may nourish her one thousand two hundred sixty days. ~ **Revelation 12:6**

The portion of the Jews that refuse to worship the image of the beast will be protected from the antichrist for three-and-a-half years. They will flee back into the wilderness. They will reside there much like when they were with Moses in the book of Exodus. The Jews will be there (in Petra) protected by God. This makes sense as the Jews fleeing Israel would

---

[35] Nathan Gopen, "Is Petra and End Times Refuge in the Wilderness", <u>Bible World Now</u>, March 5, 2017, <u>*https://bibleworldnow.org/tour-sites/item/23-is-petra-an-end-times-refuge-in-the-wilderness*</u>

not flee toward Egypt, Lebanon, Syria, or the Mediterranean Sea. They will naturally flee toward the mountains for safety reasons. Petra is located about fifty miles south of the Dead Sea and 170 miles southwest of modern Amman, Jordan. The armies of the antichrist will be coming from other directions, but not from Jordan. Evidence of this is supported in the Bible.

> He will enter also into the glorious land, and many countries will be overthrown; but these will be delivered out of his hand: Edom, Moab, and the chief of the children of Ammon. ~ **Daniel 11:41**

Petra appears to be the logical location fleeing Jews would seek refuge. Petra has some unique characteristics which make it ideal for protecting the Jews during the Great Tribulation. Petra only has one entrance. The entrance is narrow (roughly ten to twenty feet wide) and long (about a mile long). Petra is also high in the mountains in rugged terrain. Petra was also one of the places God took the Israelites to in the book of Exodus. Moses struck the rocks there with his staff, bringing water from them for the Jews during the time of their Exodus from Egypt. In addition to providing Petra as a protective fortress for the Jews, God might also use other natural events (such as earthquakes) to protect the remnant of Israel that seeks His protection. The Bible says two Holy witnesses will be given power to perform miracles. I believe the witnesses will help lead the Jews out of Israel toward the relative safety of Petra. I believe fleeing Jews able to escape to the relative safety of Petra, may quote Psalm 60:9-12:

> Who will bring me into the strong city? Who has led me to Edom? Haven't you, God, rejected us? You don't go out with our armies, God. Give us help against the adversary, for the help of man is vain. Through God we will do valiantly, for it is he who will tread down our adversaries. ~ **Psalm 60:9-12**

The Bible provides evidence Petra is the place prepared for the protection of the Jewish remnant. Isaiah refers to a place in Moab called Sela, which means "rock." Petra also means rock. In fact, some English translations of the Bible use Petra in this verse instead of Sela. Petra is in the general mountainous area, which is in modern-day Jordan. Note how the passage ends with a reference to the eventual new Kingdom of Christ being established, after the outcasts of Moab are done hiding from the devastator, when the oppressor meets his end.

Send the lambs for the ruler of the land from Selah to the wilderness, to the mountain of the daughter of Zion. For it will be that as wandering birds, as a scattered nest, so will the daughters of Moab be at the fords of the Arnon. Give counsel! Execute justice! Make your shade like the night in the middle of the noonday! Hide the outcasts! Don't betray the fugitive! Let my outcasts dwell with you! As for Moab, be a hiding place for him from the face of the destroyer. For the extortionist is brought to nothing. Destruction ceases. The oppressors are consumed out of the land. **A throne will be established in loving kindness. One will sit on it in truth, in the tent of David, judging, seeking justice, and swift to do righteousness.** *[emphasis added]* - **Isaiah 16:1-5**

Jesus indicated the place of refuge to be in the mountains (Matthew 24:16). The passage in the book of Revelation places the location to be in the desert (or wilderness). Petra matches the description of a desert in the mountains. The Jews that refuse to bow down and worship the image of the beast will serve as a witness to those remaining on the earth during the Great Tribulation. For those being protected in Petra at this time they may find encouragement from the Psalms.

Be still, and know that I am God. I will be exalted among the nations. I will be exalted in the earth." - **Psalm 46:10**

God will directly protect the remnant of the Jewish population in Petra. God will also provide His two holy witnesses to deliver a message of repentance. The two holy witnesses and the Jewish refugees will be witnessing to the rest of the world. They will be protected by God during their ministry. During the Great Tribulation, we are to go immediately into the wilderness. We are to simply trust in God to provide for all our daily needs. The Bible tells us God will care for us. He will nourish us in the wilderness. At this time the battle will not be ours to fight. God will be fighting the battle on our collective behalf while we stay safely protected by the Lord in the wilderness. The remnant of the Jewish population will be cared for in the caves of Petra. We serve a God who is the very essence of love. At this time, we must have faith in His ability to care for us. He will nurture us during the Great Tribulation.

THE END OF THE AGE

As he sat on the Mount of Olives, the disciples came to him privately, saying, "Tell us, when will these things be? What is the sign of your coming, and of the end of the age?" Jesus answered them, "Be careful that no one leads you astray. For many will come in my name, saying, 'I am the Christ,' and will lead many astray. You will hear of wars and rumors of wars. See that you aren't troubled, for all this must happen, but the end is not yet. For nation will rise against nation, and kingdom against kingdom; and there will be famines, plagues, and earthquakes in various places. But all these things are the beginning of birth pains. "Then they will deliver you up to oppression and will kill you. You will be hated by all of the nations for my name's sake. Then many will stumble, and will deliver up one another, and will hate one another. Many false prophets will arise and will lead many astray. Because iniquity will be multiplied, the love of many will grow cold. But he who endures to the end will be saved. This Good News of the Kingdom will be preached in the whole world for a testimony to all the nations, and then the end will come. ~ **Matthew 24:3-14**

MATTHEW'S GOSPEL RECORDS THIS DIALOG between Jesus and His disciples. Jesus' disciples wanted to know what to expect as they approach the end of the age. Jesus answers their question. This is His direct testimony (we can have certainty in what He says will take place). First, Jesus spells out things we can expect to happen as we approach the end of the age. They include:

- Many will come in His name (these are false prophets).
- You will hear of wars and rumors of wars.
- Nation will rise against Nation.
- Kingdom will rise against Kingdom.
- Famines will occur in various places.
- Earthquakes will occur in various places.
- You may be handed over and persecuted for your testimony in Him.

- You may be hated because of your testimony in Him.
- The love of most will grow cold.
- Many will turn away from the faith and betray and hate one another.

After spelling out the above list of things we can expect to take place as we approach the final days Jesus provides a list of things that will be a direct outcome of these events as follows:

- The one who stands firm to the end will be saved.
- This gospel of the kingdom will be preached in the whole world.
- A testimony will be provided to All Nations.
- The end will come.

What we can take from the above lists of items is that God has promised those who stand firm in their faith in the truth of God's holy word will be saved. Even if they face persecution, or even martyrdom, if they stand firm in their faith they will be saved in the end and will live in eternity with their loving God. We can be assured God will bring *ultimate* good for those who seek Him because the first item on the list of outcomes says, "The one who stands firm to the end will be saved." Note that this promise speaks to our eternal state. We may be asked to suffer and face persecution in this present world, but God promises the ultimate good in our eternal state in this promise. Saved Christians will carry the gospel of His Kingdom to all nations. Christians won't use threats, manipulation, or coercion to deliver His message. They will deliver the message from their hearts in love. The outcome is His testimony will be preached to all nations. The final item on the list of outcomes is "The end will come." Things in the world will have become so wicked during these final days that God's most merciful act will be to bring it to an end for His true believers. Think about that for a moment. That should get you excited to try to make a difference in the world today. We are to be the hands and feet of God to make things better. We are to be active! We are to work as hard as we can to bring this about in these final days. Now, let's look at the middle part of what Jesus told His disciples in response to their question. As this dialogue continues, we clearly see the final three-and-a-half years known as the Great Tribulation.

When, therefore, you see the abomination of desolation, which was spoken of through Daniel the prophet, standing in the holy

place (let the reader understand), then let those who are in Judea flee to the mountains. Let him who is on the housetop not go down to take out the things that are in his house. Let him who is in the field not return back to get his clothes. But woe to those who are with child and to nursing mothers in those days! Pray that your flight will not be in the winter nor on a Sabbath, for then there will be great suffering, such as has not been from the beginning of the world until now, no, nor ever will be. Unless those days had been shortened, no flesh would have been saved. But for the sake of the chosen ones, those days will be short-ened. "Then if any man tells you, 'Behold, here is the Christ!' or, 'There!' don't believe it. For there will arise false Christ's, and false prophets, and they will show great signs and wonders, so as to lead astray, if possible, even the elect. "Behold, I have told you beforehand. "If therefore they tell you, 'Behold, he is in the wilderness,' don't go out; or 'Behold, he is in the inner rooms,' don't believe it. For as the lightning flashes from the east, and is seen even to the west, so will the coming of the Son of Man be."
~ **Matthew 24:15-27**

What Jesus is saying here is in those final days we are to trust God fully. We are not to go back into our homes to even get a cloak. We are to flee to the wilderness and simply trust Him. At this point things will be so bad they will not be within our control. Jesus says He will take care of you. The above Bible verses are specifically speaking to those in Judah, but all Christians will be directed to fully trust in God for their protection during these times. God will direct His two holy witnesses to deliver a message of repentance to the world's population at this time. The remnant of the nation of Israel will also be used as a witness to the remaining population of the earth as they remain protected by God in the wilderness (a place prepared in advance for their protection). They will be delivering a message of repentance to the earth and will also be communicating the earthly population should reject the antichrist. The above Bible verses also speak to the importance of prayer during this time. We should be praying for those in Judah during the Great Tribula-tion. We are simply asked to pray and trust Him to protect us. The set of Bible verses go on to say Jesus is merciful, He will cut these days short, for the sole benefit of His elect people. A final warning is issued saying,

"You will hear lies from the false prophet." You are to recognize those lies for what they are. You are to simply ignore them. Allow Jesus to protect you in the wilderness. These Bible verses tell you His second coming will be clear as day is from night. His appearance in the sky will be miraculous (it can't be mistaken). Jesus is being merciful to you now by communicating this to you because the Bible says the false prophet will be provided the power to perform miraculous signs that make him appear to be the Messiah. Take strength. Know you have the truth. Trust in what the Bible tells you. Jesus says something very interesting to His disciples in the final portion of this set of verses:

> For wherever the carcass is, that is where the vultures gather together. "But immediately after the suffering of those days, the sun will be darkened, the moon will not give its light, the stars will fall from the sky, and the powers of the heavens will be shaken; and then the sign of the Son of Man will appear in the sky. Then all the tribes of the earth will mourn, and they will see the Son of Man coming on the clouds of the sky with power and great glory. He will send out his angels with a great sound of a trumpet, and they will gather together his chosen ones from the four winds, from one end of the sky to the other."' ~ **Matthew 24:28-31**

The image of the carcass and vultures indicates something is dying or is already dead. Vultures only feed on dead carcasses. These Bible verses represent the spiritual decay present on the earth at the time of the Great Tribulation. The most applicable description will be of a dead carcass. The vultures circling the carcass may also point to demonic forces being unleashed specifically at this time on earth. The verses conclude with the triumphant return of Jesus. Things will have become so bad in those last three-and-a-half years that Jesus' return will be seen as a merciful option by our loving God to cut those days short for His elect. At this point in time, He's waited until the absolute last moment to allow as many as possible enough time to repent and turn to Him for their salvation. He's provided every possible opportunity to draw His people back to Him. Nobody knows exactly when the Return of Jesus will take place, but one thing we can all be assured of is folks remaining on earth at this time should have been able to recognize their need for a savior. Jesus would have sent them numerous signs that would have followed the exact progression laid out within the pages of the Bible. He would have sent many warning signs including world wars, natural disasters, and signs in the heavens. He would have permitted the killing of all the life in the oceans by this point. The bottom line: if you don't recognize your need for a savior, you can't honestly blame God!

You can trust God to look out for you in a loving manner. He may allow things to test us, but He promises He works all things for the ultimate good for those that believe in Him (and again, here we are talking about your eternal state). Further, He says when we are permitted to go through trials and tribulation, He will use those experiences to refine us, so we are as pure as refined gold. As a loving father provides discipline for their children, God will also discipline us. We should expect God to correct us when we start to walk away from Him, but we can be assured He will correct us in a loving manner. This current age is meant to provide experiences for us with the goal of refining us. The current age is meant to prepare us for living in eternity with a God who is perfect love. God never promised this life would be easy, but He promises once we accept Him as our savior, He will lead us, guide us, and protect us. He promises He will work all things for our ultimate good.

JESUS' SECOND COMING

WHEN THE ANTICHRIST SETS HIMSELF up to be worshiped in the courtyard of the temple, many Jews will rebel against him. They will not accept him as their messiah. The antichrist will mobilize all nations he controls against all organized religions on earth, but his main focus will be against Jews and Christians. The antichrist will come against Israel and seek to destroy as many Jews as possible. This will be spiritual warfare between the remaining true believers, the antichrist, and the false prophet. This will usher in the second coming of Jesus. The antichrist and false prophet will seek to destroy the word of God as well as any people remaining on earth loyal to the truth of the Lord and His true word. The moment Jesus returns is when Satan, the beast, and the false prophet are captured and thrown into the lake of fire. Revelation chapter 20 provides an account of the defeat of Satan, the antichrist, and the false prophet.

> And after the thousand years, Satan will be released from his prison, and he will come out to deceive the nations which are in the four corners of the earth, Gog and Magog, to gather them together to the war; the number of whom is as the sand of the sea. They went up over the width of the earth, and surrounded the camp of the saints, and the beloved city. Fire came down out of heaven from God and devoured them. The devil who deceived them was thrown into the lake of fire and sulfur, where the beast and the false prophet are also. They will be tormented day and night forever and ever. ~ **Revelation 20:7-10**

The picture painted in these Bible verses is the final battle of Armageddon and the final judgment of Satan, the antichrist, and the false prophet. Satan will have been released from his bondage and will be thrown down to earth where he will seek to do battle against God and His saints. Toward the end of the great tribulation, they will gather themselves against the remaining saints of the earth and against God and His armies near the holy city to do battle against God and His saints. They will be swiftly defeated by God in a supernatural manner. This will occur at the second coming of Jesus at the very end of the age. Jesus and His armies will defeat Satan and His followers during this final battle of Armageddon.

The Bible provides many explicit details concerning the return of Jesus. To understand the full truth and specific details of His return we should take a look at scriptures within the Bible that paint a vivid picture of the details concerning Jesus' return during His second coming.[36] Jesus route of return is detailed in Isiah 16:1, which states, "Send the lambs for the ruler of the land from Selah to the wilderness, to the mountain of the daughter of Zion." This is a prophecy telling us Jesus is going to return to Jerusalem "from Sela" (Petra) by way of "the wilderness" (the same "wilderness" Israel wandered in 3,500 years ago when they left Egypt). The fact the Lord will return by this exact route is verified by such passages as Isaiah 63:1-6, Ezekiel 20:33-38, 39:11, Micah 2:12-13, and Habakkuk 3:3. The mention of Edom, Bozrah, and Teman in these passages is highly significant. Petra was the southern capital of the ancient land of Edom, and Bozrah was the northern capital of ancient Edom. Teman was an area in ancient Edom comparable to what we now refer to as a "state" or "territory." All these places are in modern Jordan. All these passages make it clear this is the exact route the Lord is going to follow when He returns to Jerusalem at His actual second coming. When Christ returns to this earth, He is first going to the Jews in Petra. There He will reveal Himself to them "face to face," Ezekiel 20:33-38. This is where Zechariah 12:10 and 13:6 fit into the prophetic picture. The first passage clearly states, "… and they will look to me whom they have pierced; and they shall mourn for him, as one mourns for his only son, and will grieve bitterly for him, as one grieves for his firstborn." (See also Revelation 1:7.)

One might ask, why should the Jews go into mourning when they finally look upon the Lord? The answer to this question is the religious Jews who believe the promises of a coming Messiah set forth in their Torah (Deuteronomy 18:15-19), do not know the identity of their promised Messiah. While they believe the promises of God in the Old Covenant and are actually "looking for" their Messiah to come, they do not believe their promised Messiah is the Lord Jesus Christ, the Savior of New Testament believers. What a shock it will be for the Jewish remnant in Petra when the Lord appears in their midst, "One will say to him, 'What are these wounds between your arms?' Then he will answer, 'Those with which I was wounded in the house of my friends.'" Zechariah 13:6

---

[36]   "Israel's flight to Petra & then Home Again", Angels on Assignment, March 24, 2010, *https://angelsonassignment.org/petra.html*

(compare John 15:12-15). The Jews will then finally realize their Messiah is the very same Lord Jesus Christ whom their Jewish forefathers rejected and crucified so long ago. After the Lord identifies Himself to the Jews in Petra, He will then lead the Jews out of Petra headed back for their homeland, and their beloved city of Jerusalem, exactly as set forth in Micah 2:12-13. Verse 12 plainly speaks about the Jewish "remnant" being gathered to the land of ancient Edom (Bozrah or Petra) in much commotion. Compare this with Isaiah 16:2-4 and Psalm 108:7-11. But verse 13 speaks about them leaving Petra headed back home. Notice the marching order clearly set forth in this verse. The Lord Himself will lead them out of Petra. Micah 2:13 says, "He who breaks open the way goes up before them. They break through the gate and go out. And their king passes on before them, with Yahweh at their head." Compare Psalm 108:11. Immediately following the Lord will be their king. As the Jews leave Petra, they will follow their king out of Petra who will follow the Lord Himself.

When the Lord steps out from the cleft in the rock (the narrow valley) exit from Petra opening on to the desert floor, immediately He will be confronted with the hordes of wicked men who will have assembled there to overwhelm and destroy the Jews in Petra. The battle of Armageddon will have begun! The prophet Isaiah saw this battle in a vision given to him centuries ago by the Lord Isaiah 63:1 says, "Who is this who comes from Edom, with dyed garments from Bozrah? Who is this who is glorious in his clothing, marching in the greatness of his strength? It is I who speak in righteousness, mighty to save." Isaiah 63:2 then says, "Why is your clothing red, and your garments like him who treads in the wine vat?" (Compare Revelation 14:19-20). Revelation 19:11-13 says, "I saw the heaven opened, and behold, a white horse, and he who sat on it is called Faithful and True. In righteousness he judges and makes war. His eyes are a flame of fire, and on his head are many crowns. He has names written and a name written which no one knows but he himself. He is clothed in a garment sprinkled with blood. His name is called "The Word of God." (Compare Revelation 19:11-13). Isaiah 63:4 says, "For the day of vengeance was in my heart, and the year of my redeemed has come." (Compare Isaiah 61:1-3). Isaiah 63:3-6 says, "I have trodden the wine press alone. Of the peoples, no one was with me. Yes, I trod them in my anger and trampled them in my wrath. Their lifeblood is sprinkled on my garments, and I have stained all my clothing. For the day of vengeance was in my heart, and the year of my redeemed has come. I looked, and there was no one to help; and I wondered that there was no one to uphold. Therefore my own arm brought salvation to me. My own wrath upheld me. I trod down the peoples in my anger." This mighty battle against His enemies and the enemies of Israel will be fought by the Lord all the way through the wilderness right up the east side of the Dead Sea. Compare Ezekiel 38:21-23, 39:1-8, Zechariah 14:1-15, and Revelation 19:11-21. This will be a real, literal battle proven by the fact that when Isaiah saw the Lord, he marveled that His clothing was stained red. This truth is also verified in Revelation 19:13.

There are other details about this final battle that can be found in many other Scriptures in God's Word. For instance, Psalm 110:5-7 says, "The Lord is at your right hand. He will crush kings in the day of his wrath. He will judge among the nations. He will heap up dead bodies. He will crush the ruler of the whole earth. He will drink of the brook on the way; therefore he will lift up his head." This Bible verse speaks about this same final end-time battle, even seeing he will drink from a brook on the way. A look at a map of the area reveals about halfway up the east side of the Dead Sea is the Arnon river. This Scripture tells us the Lord will pause at that river and drink, and when He drinks from it He will be refreshed. This little detail clearly points to the fact that when Jesus returns, He will return fully human, but in His resurrected form, just as when He visited his disciples immediately after He had been resurrected and returned to them several times.

The Lord, just as Joshua did some 3,400 years ago, will lead the Jews through "the wilderness" on the east side of the Dead Sea and back to their beloved homeland. When they arrive at the north end of the Dead Sea, the Lord will then turn due west and lead them across the Jordan river. Some 3,400 years ago when the soles of the feet of the priests bearing the Ark of the Covenant stepped into the waters of the Jordan, it parted, and the Jewish people passed across the Jordan on dry land. Joshua 3 and 4 provide details. I suspect when the Lord steps into the Jordan, it will part again just like it did 3,400 years ago and the Jewish people will once more cross over on dry land. The Lord will then lead the Jews from the Jordan westward on towards Jerusalem. This will bring the Lord and the whole company of Jews back into Jerusalem directly over top of the mount of Olives, fulfilling Zechariah 14:1-15. We should read this full set of Bible verses.

Behold, a day of Yahweh comes, when your plunder will be divided within you. For I will gather all nations against Jerusalem to battle; and the city will be taken, the houses rifled, and the women ravished. Half of the city will go out into captivity, and the rest of the people will not be cut off from the city. Then Yahweh will go out and fight against those nations, as when he fought in the day of battle. His feet will stand in that day on the Mount of Olives, which is before Jerusalem on the east; and the Mount of Olives will be split in two, from east to west, making a very great valley. Half of the mountain will move toward the north, and half of it toward the south. You shall flee by the valley of my mountains; for the valley of the mountains shall reach to Azel; yes, you shall flee, just like you fled from before the earthquake in the days of Uzziah king of Judah. Yahweh my God will come, and all the holy ones with you. It will happen in that day, that there will not be light, cold, or frost. It will be a unique day which is known to Yahweh; not day, and not night; but it will come to pass, that at evening time there will be light. It will happen in that day, that living waters will go out from Jerusalem: half of them toward the eastern sea, and half of them toward the western sea. It will be so in summer and winter. Yahweh will be King over all the earth. In that day Yahweh will be one, and his name one. All the land will be made like the Arabah, from Geba to Rimmon south of Jerusalem; and she will be lifted up, and will dwell in her place, from Benjamin's gate to the place of the first gate, to the corner gate, and from the tower of Hananel to the king's wine presses. Men will dwell therein, and there will be no more curse; but Jerusalem will dwell safely.

At that very time another "remnant" of Jews who did not flee to Petra will be backed up against the mount of Olives fighting for their lives, about to be overwhelmed and destroyed by the armies of the Antichrist. At that precise time the Lord Jesus Christ will come over top of the mount of Olives. Those embattled Jews will look up and see their promised Messiah coming to save them, and will cry out with a mighty shout, "Blessed is He that cometh in the name of the Lord," Matthew 23:39. At that exact instant the entire mountain will split wide open, creating a valley and an escape route for those embattled Jews. They will flee through the valley to safety, while the Lord rages into their enemies, trampling them under His feet and filling the Kidron valley with their blood " (Even unto the horse bridles), Revelation 14:20. Once Jerusalem has been secured by the Lord and those who are accompanying Him, the Lord will then proceed right on northward through the valleys of Jezreel, Achan (Achor), Jehoshaphat, and Megiddo, slaughtering His enemies all the way until He emerges right out on to the plain of Megiddo. There on the plain of Megiddo the last shot ever fired in battle, the last command of the war mongers, the last scream of the wounded and dying, will forever fade away as the blessed silence of peace settles over the whole bloody scene. Micah 4:3 then says, "and he will judge between many peoples, and will decide concerning strong nations afar off. They will beat their swords into plowshares, and their spears into pruning hooks. Nation will not lift up sword against nation, neither will they learn war anymore." This Bible verse promises the vision that many have of world peace. You can see here the Bible clearly promises at some point we will have world peace, but we can see that is only possible through accepting Jesus Christ as our lord and savior and allowing Him to reside as king over the entire world. Until that time, we are called as Christians to accept Jesus as our lord and savior and to allow Him to be lord over our lives while we wait for this promise of world peace to be fulfilled. The only way we can do that in our own lives, is to place Jesus, our king, directly at the center of our lives.

After the final judgment of mankind takes place, as noted above, the new heaven and new earth will be ushered in. The new Jerusalem will come down from heaven, and Jesus rules with mankind on earth. Revelation 21 paints for us a picture of a new Heaven and a new Earth:

> I saw a new heaven and a new earth: for the first heaven and the first earth have passed away, and the sea is no more. I saw the holy city, New Jerusalem, coming down out of heaven from God, prepared like a bride adorned for her husband. I heard a loud voice out of heaven saying, "Behold, God's dwelling is with people, and he will dwell with them, and they will be his people, and God himself will be with them as their God. He will wipe away every tear from their eyes. Death will be no more; neither will there be mourning, nor crying, nor pain, anymore. The first things have passed away." He who sits on the throne said, "Behold, I am making all things new." He said, "Write, for

these words of God are faithful and true." He said to me, "I am the Alpha and the Omega, the Beginning and the End. I will give freely to him who is thirsty from the spring of the water of life. He who overcomes, I will give him these things. I will be his God, and he will be my son. But for the cowardly, unbelieving, sinners, abominable, murderers, sexually immoral, sorcerers, idolaters, and all liars, their part is in the lake that burns with fire and sulfur, which is the second death." ~ **Revelation 21:1-8**

When Jesus returns in His second coming, He will usher in His kingdom here on earth. The entire universe will be modified in an instant. Think about that for a moment. God is going to modify the entire universe so that He can reside with you. What an amazing thought! God also says while everything else will be destroyed His word will never pass away. This passage goes on to describe the bride of Christ and a Marriage Supper of the Lamb:

One of the seven angels who had the seven bowls, who were loaded with the seven last plagues came, and he spoke with me, saying, "Come here. I will show you the wife, the Lamb's bride." He carried me away in the Spirit to a great and high mountain, and showed me the holy city, Jerusalem, coming down out of heaven from God, having the glory of God. Her light was like a most precious stone, as if it were a jasper stone, clear as crystal; having a great and high wall; having twelve gates, and at the gates twelve angels; and names written on them, which are the names of the twelve tribes of the children of Israel. On the east were three gates; and on the north three gates; and on the south three gates; and on the west three gates. The wall of the city had twelve foundations, and on them twelve names of the twelve Apostles of the Lamb. He who spoke with me had for a measure a golden reed to measure the city, its gates, and its walls. The city is square, and its length is as great as its width. He measured the city with the reed, twelve thousand twelve stadia. Its length, width, and height are equal. Its wall is one hundred forty-four cubits, by the measure of a man, that is, of an angel. The construction of its wall was jasper. The city was pure gold, like pure glass. The foundations of the city's wall were adorned with all kinds of precious stones. The first foundation was jasper;

> the second, sapphire; the third, chalcedony; the fourth, emerald; the fifth, sardonyx; the sixth, sardius; the seventh, chrysolite; the eighth, beryl; the ninth, topaz; the tenth, chrysoprase; the eleventh, jacinth; and the twelfth, amethyst. The twelve gates were twelve pearls. Each one of the gates was made of one pearl. The street of the city was pure gold, like transparent glass. I saw no temple in it, for the Lord God, the Almighty, and the Lamb, are its temple. The city has no need for the sun or moon to shine, for the very glory of God illuminated it, and its lamp is the Lamb. The nations will walk in its light. The kings of the earth bring the glory and honor of the nations into it. Its gates will in no way be shut by day (for there will be no night there), and they shall bring the glory and the honor of the nations into it so that they may enter. There will in no way enter into it anything profane, or one who causes an abomination or a lie, but only those who are written in the Lamb's book of life." ~ **Revelation 21:9-27**

Earlier in the New Testament, Jesus gave us the assurance that we can depend on his words, both now, and for what is to come:

> Heaven and earth will pass away, but my words will not pass away. ~ **Matthew 24:35**

The reason His word won't pass away is His word (the Holy Bible) attests to God's very nature. Everything contained within the Bible delivers a single consistent message of how God chose to create our universe and how He chose to work to draw mankind back to Him after their fall in the Garden of Eden. When even the universe He created passes away His word will remain consistent. God chose to create you, He chose to love you, He chose to give you a role to play in His creation and redemption story. He chose to re-make the entire universe so He could finally come back and be with you for eternity. He is only coming back to save those who are redeemed via the choice they made to openly accept the free offer made by Jesus Christ. Jesus took the burden of your sins upon himself. The choice is yours. I know my choice and pray you would also seek salvation in Jesus for your sins. God loves you. He is love!

THE FATE OF THE WICKED

THE BIBLE STATES THE WAGES of sin is death. As a result, we can be assured mankind is currently living with a death sentence. All have sinned and fallen short of the glory of God. A picture of the final judgment of mankind is presented in Revelation chapter 14. It is worth reading the entire chapter in full:

> I saw, and behold, the Lamb standing on Mount Zion, and with him a number, one hundred forty-four thousand, having his name, and the name of his Father, written on their foreheads. I heard a sound from heaven, like the sound of many waters, and like the sound of a great thunder. The sound which I heard was like that of harpists playing on their harps. They sing a new song before the throne, and before the four living creatures and the elders. No one could learn the song except the one hundred forty-four thousand, those who had been redeemed out of the earth. These are those who were not defiled with women, for they are virgins. These are those who follow the Lamb wherever he goes. These were redeemed by Jesus from among men, the first fruits to God and to the Lamb. In their mouth was found no lie, for they are blameless.

THE THREE ANGELS

> I saw an angel flying in mid heaven, having an eternal Good News to proclaim to those who dwell on the earth, and to every nation, tribe, language, and people. He said with a loud voice, "Fear the Lord, and give him glory; for the hour of his judgment has come. Worship him who made the heaven, the earth, the sea, and the springs of waters!" Another, a second angel, followed, saying, "Babylon the great has fallen, which has made all the nations to drink of the wine of the wrath of her sexual immorality." Another angel, a third, followed them, saying with a great voice, "If anyone worships the beast and his image, and receives a mark on his forehead, or on his hand, he also will drink of the wine of

the wrath of God, which is prepared unmixed in the cup of his anger. He will be tormented with fire and sulfur in the presence of the holy angels, and in the presence of the Lamb. The smoke of their torment goes up forever and ever. They have no rest day and night, those who worship the beast and his image, and whoever receives the mark of his name. Here is the perseverance of the saints, those who keep the commandments of God, and the faith of Jesus." I heard a voice from heaven saying, "Write, 'Blessed are the dead who die in the Lord from now on.'" "Yes," says the Spirit, "that they may rest from their labors; for their works follow with them." I looked, and saw a white cloud, and on the cloud one sitting like a son of man, having on his head a golden crown, and in his hand a sharp sickle. Another angel came out of the temple, crying with a loud voice to him who sat on the cloud, "Send your sickle, and reap; for the hour to reap has come; for the harvest of the earth is ripe!" He who sat on the cloud thrust his sickle on the earth, and the earth was reaped. Another angel came out of the temple which is in heaven. He also had a sharp sickle. Another angel came out from the altar, he who has power over fire, and he called with a great voice to him who had the sharp sickle, saying, "Send your sharp sickle, and gather the clusters of the vine of the earth, for the earth's grapes are fully ripe!" The angel thrust his sickle into the earth, and gathered the vintage of the earth, and threw it into the great wine press of the wrath of God. The wine press was trodden outside of the city, and blood came out of the wine press, even to the bridles of the horses, as far as one thousand six hundred stadia."

A picture of the fate of the beast and false prophet is presented in Revelation chapter 19:

I saw the heaven opened, and behold, a white horse, and he who sat on it is called Faithful and True. In righteousness he judges and makes war. His eyes are a flame of fire, and on his head are many crowns. He has names written and a name written which no one knows but He himself. He is clothed in a garment sprinkled with blood. His name is called "The Word of God." The armies which are in heaven followed him on white horses, clothed in white, pure, fine linen. Out of his mouth proceeds a sharp, double-edged sword, that with it he should strike the nations. He will rule them with an iron rod. He treads the wine press of the fierceness of the wrath of God, the Almighty. He has on his garment and on his thigh a name written, "KING OF KINGS, AND LORD OF LORDS." I saw an angel standing in the sun. He cried with a loud voice, saying to all the birds that fly in the sky, "Come! Be gathered together to the great supper of God, that you may eat the flesh of kings, the flesh of captains, the flesh of mighty men, and the flesh of horses and of those who sit on them, and the flesh of all men, both free and slave, small and great." I saw the beast, and the kings of the earth, and their armies, gathered together to make war against him who sat on the horse, and against his army. **The beast was taken, and with him the false prophet who worked the signs in his sight, with which he deceived those who had received the mark of the beast and those who worshiped his image. These two were thrown alive into the lake of fire that burns with sulfur.** *[emphasis added]* The rest were killed with the sword of him who sat on the horse, the sword which came out of his mouth. So all the birds were filled with their flesh." - **Revelation 19: 11-21**

This passage speaks to the actual harvest, which will be conducted by God's angels at the time of the final judgment of mankind.

I understand there are multiple Christian doctrines that speak to what the outcome of this final judgment might mean for the wicked. Some argue the outcome for the wicked will be eternal suffering in Hell along with Satan and his demons. Others (the Annihilationist) argue those that did not accept Jesus as their savior will have their bodies thrown into the fires of Hell and they will be destroyed (annihilated) but they will not suffer for an eternity in Hell. I don't believe God has fully answered this question for us as to what His perfect justice will look like at the end of the age. Furthermore, I don't believe our minds would be able to comprehend what God's perfect justice might look like. The Bible makes it clear, however, those that chose not to accept Jesus as their savior will be forever separated from God. They will never enter the presence of their loving God. What a tragic outcome for their lives! The important thing is for those of us who have accepted salvation we should have no fear of this final judgment. We were not meant to serve God in fear. We are meant to serve God in love. Perfect love casts out all fear.

> He will wipe away every tear from their eyes. Death will be no more; neither will there be mourning, nor crying, nor pain, anymore. The first things have passed away. ~ **Revelation 21:4**

> There will in no way enter into it anything profane, or one who causes an abomination or a lie, but only those who are written in the Lamb's book of life. ~ **Revelation 21:27**

God has made it clear only those whose names have been written in the Lamb's book of life will enter His presence for eternity, and He will wipe away the tears of all who have accepted Him as their savior once the old order has passed away. We must trust God that He is Love, He is righteous, and His justice is perfect. We must understand God's judgment on the lost souls is a direct result of those souls not accepting the free offer of salvation He has made available for them. The consequence of the judgment is theirs, and only theirs, to bear. God is completely innocent of this judgment against these souls. God is a patient God. He has provided everyone an entire lifetime to accept His gift of salvation, but He is also a God of perfect justice. He cannot tolerate sin to go unpunished. It doesn't benefit us, as sinful humans, to think we have a greater sense of justice than God. We must trust God's justice in full. We must accept His justice will be perfect and is currently incomprehensible to us. The important thing is we accept His gift of salvation so we can serve Him without fear.